POWER TOWN

Democracy
Discarded

Doris Shackleton

McCLELLAND AND STEWART

ISBN: 0-7710-8100-6 (cloth)

McClelland and Stewart Limited,
The Canadian Publishers,
25 Hollinger Road,
Toronto Ontario.
M4B 3G2

Printed and bound in Canada
by John Deyell Company

Contents

To the memory of some talks
with Ron Shackleton, LL.B.

Preface

Today in Canada there is a distinct sense of being stymied, reduced to immobility, by the federal government's actions and attitudes toward people of all regions. The cleft has widened between us and them. It is far worse – we feel we have less knowledge, less power to control or direct our government – than at any time in our remembered history.

The paralysis grows. We are accepting what we should resist – the secret conduct of what can scarcely be called *public* affairs, since the public now merely suffers the results, without being taken into the confidence of those who govern.

We have an unhappy sense of having been vanquished within our own country by our own leaders. We have begun to believe there is nothing we can do to resume democratic control.

Perhaps it has been shaping for a long time, but there is a dramatic time frame within which we can look at this accelerated plunge toward unresponsive power.

It coincides with the administration of Pierre Trudeau, beginning with his successful campaign in 1968. At first his administration was at odds, while phantoms of new "participatory" democracy conflicted with very real employed techniques of centralized control. The phantoms faded, in often comic attempts to introduce experimental patterns of participation. They have been swept away like yesterday's rubbish.

In a spirit of curiosity about this reversal of 1968's great expectations, I have looked closely inside the fortress of Ottawa. People from all political parties as well as from the public service have talked to me, confirming what I sensed was happening. Most of those people don't wish to be identified. I also had the familiar experience of receiving surreptitiously copies of "confidential" government papers. I have read others, not secret but overlooked perhaps because of the innocence that saves us from expecting disasters to come our way. The conversations and the documents add up to an indictment.

I also attended the fascinating and extremely significant court case in Ottawa in July 1976 when Walter Rudnicki, a public servant, successfully sued the Central Mortgage and Housing Corporation (CMHC) for wrongful dismissal. The decisions taken by that court are far-reaching. The evidence laid bare crass tyranny, hypocrisy, and a crude attempt to get rid of a "troublemaker" who had tried to deal honestly with a client group. Surely few government machinations have been so bluntly exposed – yet the top bureaucrat of that Corporation continues to enjoy a position of power at Trudeau's right hand.

I have put together what seems to me to be a story of failure by the Trudeau government to maintain a real connection with the people. It may be that establishing such a connection is the hardest problem we now face as a nation, and the most important.

We must move consciously toward greater democracy, or swiftly and inevitably to autocracy.

I don't attempt a scientific analysis of a phenomenom in public administration. Because the only remedy is by wide understanding and concern, I'll write plainly and briefly, to be read quickly as you go about your day's affairs.

These, too, are your affairs.

1   The Spirit of '68

We have come to despise the Ottawa bureaucrat, and he feels it, and resents it.

Consider his dilemma.

His job is not the sinecure sometimes imagined, but requires, in fact, superhuman equipment, of which he is rather proud. For example he is by his seventh year exquisitely tuned to the least vibration of power. He can precisely judge the morning's breeze, to sail with the wind, or stay out of the draft. He specializes in the non-effect: he has learned ease in non-speech; presumes by non-hearing; predicts by no expectation of result. He is scientifically inclined: measures his time in man-years; computes his job-description; traces his career by threading a maze. Against stonewalls he sidesteps, or he waits. The prize at the end of the maze, like the smell of cheese, is Retirement. He arrives with no understanding of where he has been, but knowing in his heart he has done it well.

Meanwhile, Ottawa is a pretty place to call home, and his family enjoys life, safely.

So why have we all turned on the bureaucrat, and why do we berate him for his lack of either civility or service? If we only *knew*, he thinks. If we only knew what it's like to work in Ottawa today.

Right now throughout the federal civil service there is mistrust, there is unease, in such dollops that you find them in your sandwiches in the cafeteria and they drop on your page when you start to write a memo. You call *that* an easy job?

Once there were whole areas of government where good things were going forward. There was respect for an effective deputy minister, cheerful awe of the Minister in his office up top. Some sense of progress. Of direction.

Now it's lost. You can't feel that atmosphere in Ottawa today. Nobody is sure of his job – either of his tenure in it, or of what the job is.

There are mean comments, scarcely overheard. Grudges. Tension.

Basically, fear. What if Power has been mislaid? You think it's behind the closed door at the end of the hall. But the sense of trickery – how can you know whether, if you open that door, there'll be anything but a bare room?

One of the things the public servant acquires, as a result, is a defensive cunning against the customers, suckers, clients, taxpayers, you and me. Isn't the job hard *enough*, without having to tolerate a bunch of flak from the dumb mob outside?

There they go, says the public servant, there they go round and round the Eternal Flame on Parliament Hill, with their picket signs. One crude slogan changes to the next, but there's always a protest, always a demonstration. Who in hell do they think is listening?

Then sometimes when it's spring in Ottawa, after the *Globe and Mail* and the second coffee, the public servant looks out the window and expands his view and says, Migod, it's wrong. The people out there shouldn't be enemies. This is a rotten way to run a country.

In 1968 the phrase in vogue was "Participatory Democracy." It meant heightened democracy, new contacts with government. It meant a sense of government perceived and understood and owned in part by everyone who wanted to make the effort.

In 1976 we stare at the colossal machine that has been created; we don't expect to be involved. Hardly a soul now ventures to suggest the government belongs to us.

What changed?

Three things.

First, Trudeau stopped the dialogue. The Prime Minister in his own person, the man who introduced that happy phrase back in 1968. Now he is so out of tune that everything he says offends us.

Trudeau snipped the last frayed strands on Thanksgiving Day, 1975, and oddly he did so employing his preferred medium, television, his *direct contact* with the people.

Prime Minister Trudeau antagonized almost everyone who watched that night, even those who wanted wage and price controls, by his perversity. He had allowed us to think for months that he was up in a treetop communing with the summer sky; he kept on saying he did not believe in wage and price controls; we had elected him because he rejected the policy in the strongest terms. Then in October 1975 he gave us in one terse speech a precedent-shattering set of controls that bewildered and blocked the whole economic process.

If we had had some little say in that decision, we could face it better now. Instead, we remember how he looked on our screens, aged, angry and petulant. That was the night Canadians knew that democracy, the participatory kind, had become inoperative.

"Whether you want to march in the parade or not, it is just too bad, you are going to have to march," Trudeau told us.

It was an unforgiveable offence to us, that speech. No Prime Minister and no federal administration has ever before treated the Canadian people in such fashion. The worst Prime Ministers have cajoled us, paying lip service to "the will of the people"; the best have been scrupulously concerned for parliamentary authority and electoral mandate.

Like changing his socks, Trudeau flipped over from remote indolence to the imposition of a three-year program of comprehensive controls that has thwarted the process of collective bargaining for unions, and turned businessmen wary, exasperated, and drag-your-heels careful.

University of Toronto law professor J. D. Morton wrote: "It is hard to resist the conclusion that the proposed legislation and its presentation is a product of panic." What Morton decried (writing in the *Globe and Mail*, October 24, 1975) was that Trudeau chose to announce his controls over television instead of presenting them to Parliament which was due to resume sittings the following day. And nowhere in his television speech did Trudeau so much as mention that the program was subject to the approval by Parliament of a bill to be presented to it. Or subject to *our* approval, in any way, shape or form.

The sweeping controls cut across provincial rights, on the pretext of "exceptional circumstance." Actually, the economic peril was a lot more exceptional a few months before Trudeau slammed the lid. But by October 13 that year, a slight improvement was evident in the inflation rate; it had dropped from 13 to about 10.5 per cent. The Gross National Product (GNP) was showing a slight positive advance, to 4 per cent instead of the zero or negative figure we had had through the first three-quarters of that year. Housing construction was up, after a lagging performance earlier in 1975. Nor was Canada doing badly in the export of manufactured goods, despite the government's claim that uncontrolled labour demands were pricing our goods too high for the world market.

If Trudeau had held back until the new figures were in, would he have left his contingency plan on the shelf? We'll never know.

Government by caprice.

And without consultation, without dialogue, without consent.

Still in shock at the end of 1975 and the beginning of the new year, we heard Trudeau mentioning future economic trends: the "new society," the "post-control period."

Nothing too new in his musings about government regulation of the economy. Why did the Conservative party leap ten feet in the air and scream *Fascist*?

Because Prime Minister Trudeau talked of what he might do to us, not what we collectively might do, if we so willed.

Mildly surprised by the reaction to his December 28th interview, Trudeau *explained*, in the January 19 speech from a prepared text. Toward the end he said:

> The government, too, has a responsibility to use the next few years to help bring about, in discussion with Parliament

and the people, the social and economic reforms that will enable Canada to emerge from the control period with a renewed sense of purpose and confidence.

That was nice. I am unable to reconcile that democratic sentiment with the paragraph that immediately followed:

The government is continuing to define its specific policy options in developing alternative ways of attacking such problems as industrial and regional growth, the price and supply of energy, labour-management relations, food policy, income distribution among individual Canadians and among regions of Canada and the relationship between government and the private sector.

Where are these policy options being formulated and defined? Deep in the bowels of government, where the first rule is, let nobody know. How can we discuss what is hidden? How can we be sure anything at all is going on behind those doors? Or that careful "policy options" prepared by public servants may not be twisted out of shape at the last minute to serve political whims, dragged out half-baked and mostly undefined, by a feverish few close to the Prime Minister? Of the "discussion with Parliament and the people" there has been no trace. There has been blunt refusal to indulge in open dialogue about the kind of economy and hence the kind of society we are to have in future.

The second cause of breakdown in democracy is the distance and the barriers we see between *us* and *them*.

What brings us through frustration to a state almost of national paralysis, is the unprecedented way that the governing coterie has set itself apart. By privilege and by secrecy.

Things are done, unashamedly, like raising the salaries of top mandarins by as much as $6000 just before the control program went into effect. Questioned, Trudeau snapped, "I don't intend to make martyrs of them."

Trudeau has increased his well-paid personally-appointed staff from the dozen or so of Pearson's time to over eighty now. And far from being frank, he is truculent about the increase, as though it were none of our affair.

In May 1975 Trudeau was questioned by the House of Commons Committee of the Whole on the costs of his establishment. Instead of a straightforward reply the Commons got a mean-spirited (and inaccurate) attack on former Conservative Prime Minister John Diefenbaker for *his* expenditures in office. The exhibition moved constant Liberal supporter Christopher Young, then editor of the Ottawa *Citizen*, to write a wrathful piece calling on the ghost of John Hampden, stout seventeenth century defender of the English Parliament's right to reject unauthorized taxation:

> Prime Minister Trudeau has evidently reached the conclusion that the normal constitutional checks and safeguards do not apply to him. The principle that the House of Commons controls the public purse does not apply. The principle that the executive is responsible to the legislature does not apply. The principle that the people have a right to know how and why their tax dollars are spent does not apply.[1]

What were the 400-odd people in the Privy Council and Prime Minister's Offices doing? Trudeau said they were "answering letters."

He refused to permit his top adviser and close friend, Michael Pitfield, secretary to the Cabinet and Clerk of the Privy Council, to appear before the House of Commons Miscellaneous Estimates Committee. Instead, the Committee had to be content with a Privy Council Office administrator, H. B. Stewart, who in answer to most questions about running the Privy Council Office said either that he didn't know or that he was not permitted to divulge the information.

Following the trend of top management in the business world, deputy ministers and other high-level government men have moved out of stuffy, sombre offices into grandeur. The new crystal palace, the head office of the Bank of Canada, was built for those very men who most sternly warn us now to restrain our spending. Wrote columnist Richard Gwyn, "Has the entire government gone mad? Is it composed of cynics,

---

[1] *Citizen*, Ottawa, May 24, 1975. p. 6.

shielded from reality by the conceit of power? Or of innocents playing let's-pretend games?"

When protests are heard against conspicuous extravagance, Trudeau swallows up the figures in the amount of government expenditures on welfare and health programs, an irritating *non sequitur*. We are not allowed the simple budgetary separation of administration costs and actual transfer payments – those sums paid out in pensions, health care, welfare, unemployment insurance – subsidies of all kinds. The cynical attempt to confuse public thinking, to conceal bureaucratic privilege, adds to our alienation.

The media can be of little help in bridging the gulf. Media people have had their egos bruised and their work made difficult because they can't get information from the tight-lipped people on Parliament Hill. Cabinet secrecy is absolute. Prime ministerial aides are fiercely protective; prime ministerial press secretaries have perfected the no-news answer.

Not long ago a W5 film crew went to Ottawa to do a story on the new-style luxury offices for cabinet ministers and deputies. They had permission to film two, but at the last minute they were phoned and told the arrangements were cancelled on direct orders from the Prime Minister. That's the kind of thing that happens all the time in Ottawa.

Besides Trudeau's irascible self, besides the secrecy and special privilege of his "group," there is a third factor that works against democracy in Ottawa today. It is perhaps the most serious and may be the hardest to reverse. It is the monolithic Liberal government structure. Party and bureaucracy separations have blurred; the government is inward-turning, all power lines lead to the centre, a centripetal force. Anyone who stands apart *really* stands apart.

The trend toward a one-party state is clear to anyone looking back over this century of predominantly Liberal party rule. The long tenure in office does not make for an open party, humbly cognizant of other people's rights.

At the same time, we've failed to get a strong call to expand the uses of democracy from the opposition parties. The Conservatives briskly quashed the leadership hopes of Flora Mac-Donald, the only candidate to talk about "the recapture by people of their own institutions and their own government." The federal New Democrats have not evoked a new democracy. Canadians act punch-drunk, our vision unfocused, our reactions dulled. Is it possible to lose interest in democracy, to lose it by chance, without noticing?

The failure of the promised extension of democracy is central to the malaise of Ottawa. The slogan is discarded as a feckless dream. The overwhelming reality is an over confident political party that snubs outside opinion, a Prime Minister who picks his private coterie, and a bureaucracy that is scared silly at the very thought of consultation.

One incident stays vivid in my mind because it says, cruelly, that people in government easily despise the people on the outside.

In the fall of 1975 the Institute of Public Administration of Canada held its 27th annual convention in Ottawa on the theme, "The Shape of Government in the 1980's." It was one of the rare occasions when both top bureaucrats and top members of the Prime Minister's staff surfaced to public view. Even Michael Pitfield was there to read a paper.

Many of the sessions received little attention in the media. In semi-private the top theorists and practitioners of public service mulled over problems, including confidentiality and accountability – too much of the first, not enough of the second. And sometimes like a ray of sunshine in a dusty room someone mentioned relating to the public at large, out there, and whether such relatedness was any concern of theirs, or ought properly to be left to the elected Members of Parliament. Fred Carrothers, president of the Institute for Research on Public Policy, roused a chuckle when he referred to citizens' groups storming the battlements, saying playfully that the sixties were the "good old days" when there were all those splendid Causes about.

At the point in the agenda graced by the presence of a Cabinet Minister, the appropriate person, President of the Treasury Board Jean Chrétien, addressed the gathering.

And no member of the press reported the moment of truth at the conclusion of his speech. A written question from an uneasy listener asked about "participatory democracy." Why doesn't it work?

Chrétien's shrug was a challenge. It *works!* he retorted. All that money, when he was Minister of Indian Affairs, poured into native organizations to help them "sock it to me." (The funding money comes not from his former department, but from the Department of the Secretary of State.)

"The trouble with these groups," cried Chrétien, "is that they want to make the decisions. If they want to make decisions let them get elected. *The truth is, some of them couldn't get elected as dog catchers!"*

From those ranks of sober senior men came sharp applause, titters of pleasure, sardonic laughter.

It left me with a very bad taste on my tongue.

Participatory democracy in the late sixties was an attempt to appease the impatience of the overcrowded urban poor and the "alienated" youth. It was given considerable impetus by people who saw it as an extension of their liberalism, and who were worried about riots in the streets.

The phrase was clumsy but its meaning obvious. Democracy means power residing in the people, who by their Yea or Nay approve or disapprove what their rulers have been doing. It only takes a vote for that much democracy. But to participate is to help formulate public policy. Not merely to confirm or reject after it's in place.

It's a very great act of faith – that men and women can govern themselves, can cooperate in various roles for collective action. Most people believe in a qualified democracy, in government delegated to those best able to govern. Inevitably there is distress, for those who do not participate are never adequately governed. Things are done to them that are unfair.

In the sixties the poor in the cities were gingerly admitted to city planning councils. The youth – that is, the students, the vocal youth – were admitted to campus administration. Presently the furore died.

But before it passed away the idea was probed and tested. Some of the hard questions were asked, but not answered. The key question is power. Participatory democracy was a proposal to subtract a little power from the centre and spread it around.

The social work fraternity took it up in a big way during the sixties, though they trembled at all its implications. "Community development" replaced casework as a method of dealing with inadequate people. It was a little like the conversion of certain Protestant churches half a century earlier from the pursuit of individual salvation to something they called the Social Gospel.

Social workers began by seeing community action as therapeutic. They described it in their jargon: "The assumption is that behavioural manifestation of the psychosocial problems of mental illness, alcohol or drug abuse are only symptomatic of a larger societal pathology, that of alienation from established norms, feelings of helplessness, hopelessness and isolation."[1]

Unfortunately the self-help neighbourhood projects kept either getting out of bounds or dying of natural causes, like frustration. When the disadvantaged couldn't be stirred to undertake the therapeutic exercise, *social animators* were turned loose to covertly guide them. Some of these *animators* took their role very seriously, and ran amuck. The Company of Young Canadians was considered a scandal, recalled for re-issue, and finally dissolved.

What most social work professionals couldn't tolerate was a real attempt by their clientele to talk back. There is nothing a doctor dislikes more than an uppity patient who diagnoses his own ailment and proposes his own remedy. There were pitiful and comic attempts to appoint welfare recipients to social work councils, there to mingle with their betters. There their defiance dwindled into surly protest and a strange, haunted look in the eye bespoke their desire to get the hell out of there.

One of the great leaders of the citizen participation movement was Saul Alinsky, head of the Chicago-based Industrial Areas Foundation. A fiendishly clever strategist, he thrust into areas of employment, urban planning and civic government, called the bluff of elitist establishment everywhere, slyly interjecting the notion that democracy means everybody in, nobody out.

Let us pause in this solemn moment of remembrance to recall words written by Edgar S. and Jean Camper Cahn:

[1]Vrooman, Paul C., M.S.W., "The Power Dilemma in Citizen Participation" *Canadian Welfare*, Ottawa. May–June 1972.

Participation constitutes . . . an exercise in the very initiative, the self-reliance, that specific programs seek to instil . . . The exhortations – *Stand on your own two feet; pull yourself up by the bootstraps; become self-sufficient; you can do it* – ring hollow when an official, by acting unilaterally, in effect officially states his lack of trust in the capacity, the instinctive reactions, the intelligence, and the sensitivity of the individual . . .

When a grown man is treated as a child with respect to those very services being rendered to him, he is unlikely to treat those services as anything more than rituals of humiliation designed either to prove his incapacity to function or to keep him dependent and out of trouble.[1]

The idea of participation was originally applied to the urban poor. It moves up the social scale as more and more of us realize how much we depend on services rendered by the public authority. The time came when only a few rich people could pay their own health costs, and health went public. Now hardly anybody can afford a house without government help. So, do we accept what is done for us, or do we look for ways to get a handle on public policy making?

The idea was at first confined to municipal government. It didn't reach into the provincial and federal levels, where the big decisions are made. Until the Liberals under Trudeau talked it up among the electorate in 1968.

Liberal strategy took up the idea of participatory democracy in the sixties. For the party, the storm signals were flying. John Diefenbaker had resurrected the failing Conservatives with a populist thrust that took him to power. He made Liberals like Louis St. Laurent and C. D. Howe look remote from the common man. So under L. B. Pearson the party decided to "get with it." Pearson was talking about the "new politics . . . based on the personal involvement of every citizen . . . " in early 1964.[2] Pearson also argued against party confrontations

[1]Cahn, Edgar S. and Jean Camper. "Citizen Participation." *Citizen Participation in Urban Development.* NTL Institute for Applied Behavioural Science. 1968. pp. 218–219.
[2]At a Liberal party banquet in Toronto, March 24, 1964.

in favour of a "national consensus," that other great idea the Liberals had about bringing in everybody (well, nearly everybody) under their party umbrella. In the third volume of his *Memoirs*, Pearson told how as far back as 1960, when in Opposition, he began recruiting new people to the party, "the beginning of our comeback." He wrote: "These meetings created a sense of participation by the rank and file and established a broad popular basis for our party. This sort of thing has its dangers of course . . . "[1]

One of the most enthusiastic purveyors of the "new politics" of "participation" was Richard Stanbury, now in the Senate, president of the Liberal party from 1968 to 1973, but at the time which he refers to as "the disaster of 1957" (when Diefenbaker was elected), a bright young lawyer and an executive member of the Liberal Association for Toronto and York. He and other eager young Liberals had come to the fore after the debacle, which he says saw the end of the old tribal customs with their party bagmen and wheeler-dealers and election night payoffs.

Pierre Elliott Trudeau also had expressed his scorn for the "old" Liberals in a much-quoted passage appearing in *Cité Libre* in 1963. It was the new wave Liberals who carried him along in his heady rush to party leadership in 1968.

So for the Liberals, the concept of "participatory democracy" meant party rejuvenation, in the first instance.

But somewhere along the line in the 1968 campaign, born in the ecstasy of Trudeaumania, the phrase was set in context as a promise to Canadians that a Liberal government would welcome them as participants in the shiny post-election world. And I think a good many, and perhaps even Trudeau himself, believed it, once the campaign directors had got out those bright posters saying "Come Work with Me," and the election leaflet on *The Just Society* which proclaimed: "Above all, it is our determined wish to make government more accessible to people, to give our citizens a sense of full participation in the affairs of government, and full control over their representatives."

[1]Pearson, L.B. *Mike. The Memoirs of the Rt. Hon. Lester B. Pearson,* Vol. 3. University of Toronto Press, 1975. p. 52.© University of Toronto Press 1975 Toronto and Buffalo.

Yet if the idea of total participatory democracy sat oddly with the Liberal party, which in fact is dominated by businessmen and lawyers with little time for other groups, it didn't suit Trudeau either. He has been, at times, an iconoclast, but never a democrat.

Consider Trudeau and the crowds in 1968. Picture again the shy smile. The gallant kisses. Kisses are not conducive to political dialogue. The flustered matron and the swooning girl were silenced except for giggles and gasps. Kisses in fact show Trudeau fending off the crowd in a roguish and winning way. It was a bit flirtatious, but there was no marriage.

The crowds – most of the crowds – adored him. And because his fresh, new image attracted a different lot of people, the impression was given of a new kind of politics.

Nothing new, of course, was happening. Thousands of people were going to the polls to vote. That was all.

The most refined analysis of the Trudeau phenomenon in the 1968 campaign came from the literary pen of Barry Callaghan, in a full three-page account in the *Telegram*.[1] He was overwhelmed with the *something new* that was happening in Canadian politics. But it stemmed from the fascination of Trudeau himself, so unlike former politicians. Callaghan wrote of Trudeau striking the pose of "the amiable aristocrat." Trudeau's basic unease with the crowd was shown in the ripping apart of a rose behind his back, during his "amiable" exchange with the pressing throng.

Trudeau's contempt for the working press (which Callaghan shared), was made clear, and also Trudeau's invariable technique in argument: to return a question, outlandishly exaggerated, to a question put to him by newsmen or audience.

Callaghan described Trudeau's speaking style, so at variance with the popular image: "There is something flat in his speeches, something ordinary." That should have been a warning of things to come – that nothing electrifying was about to happen after 1968.

Then there was the other circumstance Callaghan noted, that Trudeau in a private conversation about government, seemed to favour "some absolute system."

[1]Callaghan, Barry. "Revolution." *The Telegram,* Toronto. July 13, 1968. p. 51.

"But he may try (to institute such a system)," Callaghan wrote, "and if he systematizes government – the arrival of computer specialists with their path flow charts in the Trudeau entourage suggests he will – and at the same time tries to run it pragmatically, his fate will be that of his friend Lord Acton."

Those computer specialists were far more significant than the very ordinary sentiments that Trudeau was addressing to the nation. Once installed in the East Block, they would change Ottawa beyond recognition. But Trudeau himself? Callaghan surely exaggerated the profundity of his wisdom; that conversation about Lord Acton betrays a writer (Callaghan) much too eager to see in this new leader a great philosopher. Trudeau hasn't given us much profundity. The public speeches continue to be as ordinary as Mackenzie King at his prosiest.

Barry Callaghan witnessed the violent eruption of separatist demonstrators in LaFontaine Park on the eve of the 1968 election, and Trudeau's splendid brave defiance. Overwhelmed, Callaghan decided he could no longer tolerate the dull mediocrity of old-time Canadian politics, but must go with Trudeau, whatever the risks.

"You have a choice in life: Risk excellence with the aristocrat, or settle for safe pudding. Another forced feeding of pudding in this country and I'll choke to death. We'll all choke to death," he wrote.

Apparently vast numbers of Canadians opted for the same thrilling experience – to vote for an aristocrat. But few would have seen, as Callaghan did, the risk of despotism in that choice.

If they did, the slogan of "participatory democracy" was there to reassure them.

And it seems that Trudeau himself was affected by the excitement, and for his first term of office the fine notion of participatory democracy remained with him. He set his young men to work on the idea – those computer specialists – almost as soon as he arrived in Ottawa.

His interpretation was to let government operate from a small unit of best brains, electronically connected with the populace at large. By-passing both Parliament and the bureaucracy. Not many people saw what was happening. It began to break down – the direct communication links began to snap – within the first term of the Trudeau government.

2   The Keep

Until recently the East Block on Parliament Hill contained the offices of the Prime Minister and the Privy Council, and under Trudeau it became the strategic centre of government. No one went in without a pass. There are green baize doors to close quietly and insulate, and no bustle in the corridors.

(In 1976 the historic association of Prime Minister's Office and the old East Block is changing, with a move to more space in the Langevin Block on the opposite side of Wellington Street.)

Prime Minister Mackenzie King ran not only his office but all of External Affairs from the East Block. Each Prime Minister makes his own imprint. But at no time have there been such changes in this very central office of the executive as during Trudeau's reign.

Trudeau took office in 1968 riding the crest of an exhilarated Liberal party which had coaxed and flattered him; he took its support for granted and felt no obligation to defer to party heavyweights. Unfettered, he set out to initiate a new political style as Prime Minister and to create anew the art of government.

His impatience with the cumbersome House of Commons and its "nobody" Members was announced to the world. What was less easily seen was his equal scorn for the great grey body of the public service.

Trudeau had been employed in the Privy Council Office from 1949 to 1951; he had some first-hand acquaintance with bureaucracy at work. He considered its administrative heads mediocre, if not dull-witted. One of his earliest decisions as Prime Minister was to bring in a new breed of efficient managers to the departments as rapidly as the process of attrition would permit, through offering larger salaries and seeking to attract men from private business.

But he wasn't going to wait for the civil service to shape up. Never a man to shrink from confrontation, he created for the first time a "countervailing force" to the civil service in his own Prime Minister's Office. Through the PMO he would give direct personal leadership to the country. He would develop policy through his own advisers, his own executive group.

The move brought Cabinet Ministers under tighter prime ministerial control, while it totally demoralized the civil service. Trudeau presides over a very tame Cabinet where secrecy prevails (unlike the loose lips of the Pearson days). Though observers try to count the "hawks" and "doves" on crucial issues, no Minister really strays out of line. Continuing resignations over the past eight years have removed the independent-minded.

"Decisions in Cabinet are supposed to be reached *by consensus,*" said Paul Hellyer who resigned because his housing program was left on a back burner. "But consensus doesn't mean a majority. It means any group that includes the prime minister."

Trudeau enlarged the Cabinet, but only a few ministers have ever counted. The ministers who today show most personal strength, Donald Macdonald (Finance), Ron Basford (Justice), Jean Chrétien (Industry, Trade and Commerce), Marc Lalonde (Health and Welfare) and Otto Lang (Transport), all came into the Cabinet as Trudeau appointments, and have stayed in good repute with him. Departures and desertions make up a long and sorry list.

Trudeau's Cabinet is not at this date a powerful team. And this means that the advisers around Trudeau carry far more weight in what happens to the country than they have any right to.

After 1968 Cabinet meeting procedure was changed to require a Minister to submit policy proposals, derived through his departmental officials, (and now preferably submitted as several alternatives) to a Cabinet Committee served and guided by the top officials of the Privy Council Office. If approved, they are passed on to the whole Cabinet. The Cabinet secretariat, the PCO, is vastly enlarged, and it exercises a great deal of power as it "guides" the Cabinet toward decisions.

Although a nice distinction is supposed to exist between PCO and PMO, in practice, the lines are blurred. It has become increasingly one control centre, with a policy planning role it never had before.

Surprisingly significant and far-reaching policy decisions now emanate from this sanctum. Professor Ivan Head became Trudeau's "legislative assistant" in 1968, and has served as his personal emissary abroad (à la Kissinger). The Department of External Affairs comes close to apoplexy over this by-passing of their proper function. A recent incident was in July 1975 when an announcement from the Prime Minister's Office – without consultation with External Affairs – cancelled Canada's hosting of the United Nation's Conference on Crime, scheduled for Toronto, because the Palestine Liberation Organization was to attend.

When Pierre Juneau, having resigned the chairmanship of the CRTC, was catapulted into a Hochelaga by-election and as neatly catapulted out again by an aroused electorate, he was promptly appointed to the PMO as a "communications consultant." There was concern that his presence next to the PM meant a further downgrading of the Communications Department under the unspectacular ministership of Jeanne Sauve.

Again, a beefed-up special group in the PCO, with several new hirings in the midst of the austerity program of 1976, will "pay special attention" to the information aspects of new programs designed by the departments, because the people at the PCO think those departments aren't as good at information (public relations) as they ought to be. The strength of the departments is, again, to be diminished.

A series of documents including confidential memos relating to PMO and PCO operations gives a remarkable picture of developing changes in the executive wing of government.

First, a memo setting down, in late 1968, the four functions of the PMO:

1. The traditional role as personal secretariat, dealing with correspondence, appointments, etc;
2. A supplementary means of access to government for the unorganized public;
3. A supplementary source of non-Party political intelligence;
4. Long-term planning of government objectives to compensate for the departmental planning which is necessarily fragmented.

See in Number Two the realization of Trudeau's "participatory democracy" promises. Of the four functions, *it* was the one that failed.

The others flourished, pointing the PMO in new directions of effective power. At the same time, the Privy Council Office was moving in new parallel lines. Instead of a small, discreet group of neat grey-suited chaps who looked after the papers for Cabinet meetings and did routine things like administering oaths of office, this secretariat took on a positive role along with the PMO in initiating policy and collecting information independently from the civil service.

In a memo from Trudeau to the Cabinet in 1969, the Privy Council Office was described as evolving from the small group set up by Mackenzie King during the second World War. Its functions were now to be:

1. Secretarial;
2. Coordinating;
3. Assisting the information flow;
4. Ensuring the implementation of decisions;
5. Advisory (setting up a planning section).

As this combined expansion of the PMO and PCO in the East Block became evident in Ottawa it was described by a diligent and shocked writer as "permanently distorting the decision-making process within this nation."

In 1967, Pearson's last year in office, the PMO staff numbered twelve. By 1969 it numbered sixty. It's now eighty-two. The PMO plus the PCO numbers about 468 people. In the third volume of his *Memoirs,* former Prime Minister Pearson wrote:

> Yet, while I approve of the strengthening of the Prime Minister's and the Privy Council offices, it is disturbing to see the relative position of the civil service in Ottawa decline in relation to new administrative practices. I know that it should always be possible, as it often is wise, to insert into a civil service establishment men and women from outside, not merely because they have special qualifications but because they can bring to bear fresh insights. But if this trend becomes too pronounced, it may lead to the concentration of all power in the hands of the Prime Minister and a few chosen Ministers and advisers. Advisers and experts can work in the security of anonymity. They can also acquire a sense of power, and even delusions of grandeur, by close and continuous contact with the political leaders, without the chastening influence of exposure to fellow MPs and, inevitably, to the electors. This is a new problem of government, more complicated and more difficult than ever before, and it requires careful examination to keep it under control.[1]

In 1971 when Tom Gould of CTV questioned Trudeau about the growth of power in his office, Trudeau retorted that without such measures "you will have a lousy, weak-kneed government. And if that's the kind of thing you want, you had better elect somebody else. I just don't understand this absurd criticism of the Executive being too strong . . . "

Now the astonishing thing was that all this concentration of behind-the-scenes, responsible-only-to-us power was being created at the same time that belief in new, exciting dimensions of "participatory democracy" was being professed.

This is what Trudeau said in a press release issued on July 31, 1968:

[1]*Mike: The Memoirs of the Rt. Hon. Lester B. Pearson, Vol. 3.* University of Toronto Press, 1975. p. 94.© University of Toronto Press 1975 Toronto and Buffalo.

The Prime Minister announces the appointments of officials to his staff, at the same time outlining major changes in the organization of his office.

The Prime Minister recalled that during the recent election campaign he had repeatedly stressed the importance of increased participation by the public in the actual processes of government. He mentioned that the changes being instituted are intended to provide a greater sensitivity by government to the will of the people and to facilitate speedier decision-making and more efficient service.

To this end, the re-organization of the Prime Minister's Office will improve the Prime Minister's lines of communication with the country, as well as with Parliament, and all levels of administration. It will also ensure that the Prime Minister is able to meet the new demands placed on his office by the increased political dialogue and the complete review of many government policies promised during the election campaign.

The basic concept of the organization is that in addition to the usual Personal Assistants necessary to the discharge of his daily routine, the Prime Minister's Office should include units responsible for policy advice, for maintaining close contacts with individuals and groups in all regions of the country, for initiation of policy proposals and for information.

Among the new appointments announced that day was Pierre Levasseur, "responsible for maintaining close contacts with individuals and groups of all kinds throughout the country." Mr. Levasseur treated mere politicians with such contempt that he soon had to go; he was succeeded by David Thomson, an Alberta man, who set up meet-the-people jaunts for the Prime Minister and had to take the flak when the Prime Minister occasionally blew it, as on the memorable prairie trip when Trudeau asked farmers why he should sell their wheat.

Let's pause to look at some of the other members of the cast: they who were supposed to weld new links between people and PM.

Marc Lalonde, now Minister of Health and Welfare, was

principal secretary in 1968, the position now filled by Jim Coutts. But even more of a key figure was Jim Davey as program secretary. According to the July 1968 press release Davey's function was no less than to be "responsible for ensuring that the government and party maintain a comprehensive and coherent program and [he] will also undertake special projects from time to time at the direction of the Prime Minister for the initiation of policy proposals."

It hardly seemed necessary to have a Cabinet too. Much less a civil service.

Jim Davey was the original "total system" man. If something didn't fit into a chart it didn't exist. He had been a key worker in Trudeau's 1968 campaign and joined PMO with no previous public service experience – he had been vice president of a management consulting firm in Toronto and before that had worked for an aircraft engine manufacturing company. Just before joining Trudeau he was a project manager for Chemicell Limited, specializing in systems analysis. (In 1973 he left the PMO to help Transport Minister Jean Marchand develop a new "total system" in transportation, but in August 1975 he died after a fall.)

An assistant in 1968 to press secretary Roméo LeBlanc (now Fisheries and Environment Minister) was Vic Chapman.

(His interest in a consulting firm hired to handle press arrangements for the big federal-provincial energy conference in January 1974 led to questions about conflict of interest. Vic Chapman has now left the PMO to pursue a profitable private career with a consultant firm he calls Intertask. On the demise of Information Canada in late 1975, Intertask was handed a contract to carry out an InfoCan job of public relations for the new Anti-Inflation Board. Consulting firms such as Intertask are probably responsible for half the growth in the service sector of the Gross National Product. They sprout like mushrooms around the exit and entrance doors to the PMO.)

C. R. "Buzz" Nixon, now Defence Department deputy minister, was in charge of a "briefing room" – *not* to brief the press or the public, but a spot where little PMO groups gathered to be clued in to strategy developments.

Head and shoulders above the rest, in 1968, was Gordon

Robertson, the old pro. He was Clerk of the Privy Council and Secretary to the Cabinet, as he had been under Pearson.

(He is now PCO Secretary for Federal-Provincial Relations, but his influence has scarcely diminished. Discreet and impeccable are words coined to describe Gordon Robertson. He's a handsome man, trim and fit, with grey hair, straight black brows, a good colour. See him preside, if you have an interest in excellence, at the straining final sessions of the 1975 Conference of the Institute of Public Administration.

("Yes." He says it easily, as though he's so glad someone has thought to bring up the matter. "Yes, there are problems either way, in either vertical or horizontal decision-making. The horizontal method is slow; the vertical method may become a tunnel leading to wrong decisions. It could well be the subject of a further conference."

(He smiles, with charm. He is genuinely pleased that the question has been thus disposed of.)

Michael Pitfield (now Robertson's successor as Clerk of the Privy Council and Secretary to the Cabinet) went to the PMO in 1968 as secretary to the enormously important new Priorities and Planning Committee. Even then he swung a lot of weight. The lives and careers of many persons were in his hands. A staff person recalls Pitfield musing about where to place an individual who must be fitted in, but would need to "lose his rough edges." The individual was French-speaking but from St. Boniface, Manitoba. He was not quite *right.*

Ottawa observers were sharply suspicious of Trudeau's "Super Group." Walter Stewart saw them as remarkably similar in background, lifestyle, even appearance. They were all pragmatic in their approach to policy, he wrote, and they expected neat answers to everything. Patrick Watson went to Ottawa in early 1972 to talk to Mike Pearson about the Group. Pearson was depressed, but discreet. Watson drew his own observations however (writing in *Maclean's*) and said: "In Ottawa it's not fashionable to *care* about anything . . . The Cool Trip is much practised and totally admired . . . The guys who have developed the Cool Trip to the point of impeccable grace . . . are really dead."

Few went so far as to proclaim that Ottawa was being run by automated dead men. But it was, and is, downright uncanny to see how the PMO-PCO men copy Trudeau's personal style. Who is the man who fixes the interviewer with glistening eyes, his manner just short of weary, a cultivated "beautiful people" image, answering the uncomfortable question with the wildly exaggerated counter question: "You think there is a danger of 'co-opting' the native groups by funding them? So would you want us to cut off all grants to native people? Well, *would* you?" No, not Trudeau. Not *quite* Trudeau.

The men at the PMO and PCO by 1969 were deep into their brand-new devices to govern Canada better. A confidential document reveals a list of Priority Problems placed before the Cabinet Committee on Priorities and Planning in October, 1969. While the number one problem was "Information," the problem of "Participation" was number nine in a list of fourteen. All the problems were spelled out clearly, if simplistically. Participation was explained thus: "The problem is that existing decision-making procedures in the public and private sectors do not give those who are directly affected by the decisions made, an opportunity to contribute to the decision-making process."

But, ninth on the list, "participation" didn't look too urgent. Much more likely to get attention was the number two problem:

Public Service Personnel Management: The problem is that without greatly improved executive personnel and public service management, the government will not be able to elaborate policies and implement programs in a speedy, imaginative and progressive manner, much less gain the confidence and participation of the public service and of the public in a modern, efficient and socially sensitive government administration.

From that assessment came the "executive level" explosion.

When it reached the point of solving the problems, the document grew dim. There was some insistence that "attitudinal changes" of a high order would be needed.

"A faint Orwellian air of 1984 now hangs over the capital,"

said Peter Newman, then editor-in-chief of the Toronto *Star*, in a speech in Montreal in May 1969.

The changes in the PM's establishment were greeted with something like ecstasy by certain social scientists. York University "behavioural scientists" Fred Schindeler and C. Michael Lanphier, writing in *Canadian Public Administration* (Winter 1969) thrilled to the prospect of a Prime Minister's office using social survey techniques and attitudinal data instead of political hunches. "This modernized, dynamic institution is in a particularly advantageous position to use survey research . . . The M.P.'s no longer have a corner on the assessment of opinion at the 'grass roots' . . . " The writers felt the Prime Minister could almost get along without Parliament by these methods! At the very least, "the use of the tool by the revamped Privy Council Office and the Office of the Prime Minister . . . gives the Cabinet a new independence from the bureaucracy."

Trudeau was much taken with the "think tank" technique of aloof and isolated concentration of thought by a small group of supremely intelligent men – the very technique carried to tragic extremes in the United States where back-stage exercises in "crisis management" tried to direct the Viet Nam war operations from Washington. The technique is backed up with charts and graphs, tackling complex problems methodically with computer accuracy, and it was initiated in the United States by Robert McNamara, former U.S. defence secretary.

Following from this, also copied from the American experience, came a succession of unearthly practices called PPB (Program Planning and Budgeting), OPMS (Operational Performance Measurement Systems), MO (Management by Objectives), CBA (Cost/Benefit Analysis), and CES (Cost/Effectiveness Studies). All were introduced into the operations of the departments and agencies of our government. They were the means by which decisions were to be reached in regard to the acquisition and preservation of our national parks, the routine work of sorting mail, the cutting of forests, the distribution of family allowances. Services were to be *evaluated,* abstract things were to be *quantified.* Most government program officers lingered for months over the very first stage:

how were they to say precisely what their objectives were – as precisely, for example, as the manufacturer of toilet paper states *his* objectives?

(A former Treasury Board consultant, Professor Douglas G. Hartle, came down hard on all these techniques and processes in an address to the 1975 Public Administration Conference. Bluntly he told the bureaucrats: "The Hoover and Glassco Commissions made a fundamental error, in my opinion. They were simple minded in assuming that the techniques and processes that have proven useful in the private sector could be applied, virtually without modification, to the public sector."

(In 1975 Professor Hartle had stern words for the present prime minister:

> (In short, I hold the view that too often strong Cabinet Secretariats, elaborate Cabinet briefings prepared by these Secretariats, control over Cabinet agendas, and so on, isolate Prime Ministers and Premiers from the ultimate reality they must face. This is often done in the name of one of the techniques I have briefly discussed. To lose an election in the name of PPB, or OPMS, or MBO, and so on, is no better than to lose it in the name of insensitivity, inactivity, and indecisiveness.

(H. B. Mayo, political scientist at Carleton University, also speaks out harshly these days against the whole notion of "rational economic models" applied to government operations. An iconoclast, Mayo even says, "Why don't people frankly admit that political 'science' is a misnomer? And that politics is more art than science?")

Of course such opinions are hindsight. In 1968 political analysts were bemused, struggling to get with it, unable to predict where Trudeau's innovations would lead us.

As Trudeau appointed Task Forces, which have only to report to him, instead of Royal Commissions, which have to report publicly to Parliament, as he withheld portions of departmental studies with which he disagreed, like the recommendation for a Guaranteed Annual Income in retiring Welfare Deputy Minister Joseph Willard's 1970 report, the habit of secrecy developed thickly around the operations of the PMO and PCO.

What was actually going on was fantastic in the extreme.

In September 1970 a document was prepared for the Priorities and Planning Committee which announced in all seriousness that there was in Canada "a decreasing margin of social stability," in fact "an entropic condition tending toward chaos," requiring a change to "normative planning."

The proposition was presented in flow chart form. "Normative planning" was seen opposed to "no planning" and "linear scheduling and analysis." The latter would depend on "scheduling, administrative dexterity and intuitive brilliance," but might result in further tensions in society. "Normative planning," however, would depend on "Leadership – dedication to provide environment for people – imagination and brilliance used organically to formulate norms and values and to dialogue with people on their level – recognition of determinism and internal contradiction of existing practices and ethics; and a dedication to challenge these – recognition of entropy in existing mode; tremendous leadership energy for normative planning action – comprehensive approach to problems – degrees of freedom to operate" all ending most happily in "hope and ordered development" for society in general, and "confidence, security, relatedness" among the people.

One Cabinet minister remarked, "All this has been as intellectually stimulating as a first class university seminar – and exactly as productive," while another called the discussions "bullshit and chickenfeed."

What is noteworthy is the degree of self delusion in the same paper. An odd kind of statistical analysis was made of various measures taken in the first two years of Trudeau government, including the White Paper on Taxation; Public Housing for Low Income Groups; Indian Policy; Regional Desks at PMO; Information Canada and others. These were graded according to an "implied value" as "rational, effective, just" and so on. But no impartial judgement rated them; only the prejudiced eyes of the men in the PMO–PCO who thought they saw certain values in certain programs. On this basis there was self-congratulation on achievements to date, and the following observation:

The government is coming to the point where it will have to decide on the ideas and style of government it will present to the Canadian people at the next election. The pragmatic, careful, 'minding the shop' approach is the style that most Canadians now see in their government. The government has left the impression that it is careful and efficient and can defuse most problems before they become serious. If the government continues with this approach over the next two years, it will, in fact, be going to the people on the basis of its 'record.' Given the present political balance within the country, this may well be a successful tactic.

Remember "The Land is Strong," and the quietly satisfied, philosophic stance of Trudeau in the 1972 election? The election that missed defeating him by a hairsbreadth? The esoteric fulminations of the Prime Minister's advisers were directly responsible.

On the night of the 1972 election, Trudeau was genuinely surprised at the results. "My God, were we that bad a government?" he asked a Cabinet colleague.

Can a country be governed by charts that show that "normative planning" leads to "hope and ordered development"? Give us back Mackenzie King and his crystal ball.

During the minority government period, between 1972 and 1974, Trudeau listened to the politicians, listened to the balance-of-power New Democratic Party in Parliament. Backstage advisers were kept in a relatively minor role. Government policy was decided sometimes on the spur of the moment to save a political situation. And on *that* record they were re-elected with a whopping majority in 1974.

Rejoicing in victory, they indulged anew their addiction to flow charts and faddish techniques. "Synetics" became the rage at the Privy Council Office. It was supposed to sift from the super brains of the senior staff vitally significant base truths – by a kind of spontaneous jotting-down of inspirational thoughts. Like spirit writing?

And after 1974 Trudeau reverted to such leisurely pursuits as the "priorities exercise" which took up all the early months of 1975.

With his top Cabinet colleagues and aides he was engaged over many months in debating abstractions. A reliable leaked version of their 1975 priorities list set out five misty but laudable goals: A more just, tolerant Canadian society; Awareness of the needs of poorer nations; The distribution of people throughout the country; An evolving federal state capable of effective national action; and, finally, Sensitive, competent and responsive government at all levels. The Super Group took it from there, and the *priorities exercise* unfolded, despite growing cries that the country was in economic difficulty and there was nobody home at the Cabinet level. A further reflective encounter session was scheduled for the Cabinet at their Meach Lake retreat in early September, 1975, when Finance Minister Turner's resignation threw a spanner in the works and brought on the wage and price control program.

In the years of the Trudeau administration the key advisers within the PMO–PCO have changed very little.

Michael Pitfield has now replaced Gordon Robertson, who seemed irreplaceable. He has walked on stage, this younger man, discreet, impeccable, handsome as Robertson himself.

Pitfield differs from Robertson though when he speaks in public (a rare event). He conveys great inner tension. His arm is tight at his side, he scarcely moves his body, he reads his pages in a dull, flat voice (much as Trudeau does). At the 1975 Public Administration Institute, the civil service audience that had waited for him with a deep undercover distrust said with disappointment: "He got away without saying anything."

What he did say was that the PMO and PCO were working very well, and so were other things like the "Lambert Committee" made up of certain people from private industry (Allen T. Lambert is president of Toronto-Dominion Bank) that advises the PMO on pay rates and conditions of employment for public service executive personnel. He also said that the priorities exercise had been very useful. He remarked that "practice must be consistent with theory," and he said, at the end of his speech, "I would go further and argue that we have not viewed government sufficiently as a total system." If we were to lose sight of that totalness, he added, it could "open the way to forces that are destabilizing."

Nobody questioned him on these opinions. The neat, cool, taut, young man in the finely tailored grey suit spoke in a monotone. Afterwards written questions were handed up, and one of these asked, like a plaintive and futile cry, what was the use of forwarding policy documents from departments for Cabinet decision, when a *senior* level had the final input? Pitfield linked his hands and said, speaking modestly at first, that sometimes of course that kind of thing inevitably took place, and then his voice hardened perceptibly as he added, like an austere school-master reprimanding a delinquent scholar, that some departments "made a habit" of submitting their documents too late for consideration. Then his voice dropped back to a conciliatory tone and he said he thought the proper processes were all in place to receive position papers at the appropriate level.

In the hall, there was silence from the banks of seats where the middling-and-senior civil servants sat, and the anonymous questioner did not betray himself. But there was one youthful derisive snort of laughter, stopping abruptly – did anyone speak to *him* at coffee break next day?

Michael Pitfield's family connection is Pitfield, Mackay, Ross, investment dealers and stock brokers. He comes from Montreal and, although much younger than Pierre Trudeau, he and his wife are good friends of the Prime Minister and his wife.

As Robertson's successor as Clerk of the Privy Council he carries tremendous authority: he guides the policy operations of the entire government toward their culmination in a Cabinet decision. He is said to be tougher in group meetings than Robertson was; he lays down a position without waiting for nice feelings of consensus to develop.

During the current Parliament while Michael Pitfield has become Privy Council Clerk, Jim Coutts has become the PM's principal secretary. Coutts had worked in Pearson's office in the sixties: he is primarily a political campaign strategist. He gravitates between his firm, Canada Consulting, and the PMO, turning up whenever people are beginning to get uneasy about impending elections. He manages news and non-news with special skill: one result of his recent return was a thin scream rising from newsmen with toes pinched in the doors closed in front of them. Nobody – *nobody* – seems to get any news anymore.

To make room for Coutts, the last principal secretary, Jack Austin, a Vancouver lawyer with mining interests, one-time executive assistant to former Cabinet Minister Arthur Laing, had to be accommodated elsewhere. He had been at the PMO a year or so, but his stay had been clouded by the disclosure that he was conducting a remarkable amount of private business on the PMO letterhead, and the fact that he was still involved in a civil suit with former Vancouver business partners. He had been part of the operation in setting up Petro Canada, the government oil company announced by the minority Liberal government in 1973. Trudeau apparently had Austin slated for the post of PetroCan president, or Austin *hoped* he had. But there was a hitch. Then Energy Minister Donald Macdonald didn't want Austin. (He put in Maurice Strong, former Power Corporation president instead.)

The solution was simple. Senator Arthur Laing had died in the spring of 1975. Jack Austin was made a Senator to fill the British Columbia vacancy. In the Senate he draws a salary of $29,300 – until the age of seventy-five, when his pension starts.

The use of the Senate to confer a final reward on party stalwarts has changed, under Trudeau, only to the extent that the stalwarts look younger and younger, with many years to live well and do little, many years to devote a great deal of time to Liberal party work. Liberal party presidents are now traditionally Senators – it gives them so much free time. We have had Gildas Molgat, Richard Stanbury, and now Al Graham, all in the Senate. Keith Davey had been the party's National Director when it made its successful comeback against Diefenbaker; he went forthwith to the Senate, but he also masterminded Trudeau's successful 1974 campaign. And we are treated at times to murky glimpses of other Liberal Senators at work, like Louis Guiguere the party fund-raiser – all finding time for these little duties when not immersed in the hot thrust and parry of the old Senate Chamber.

A later arrival at the PMO is Richard O'Hagan as information and communications adviser. O'Hagan had also worked with Pearson, and is ripe with political wisdom. The reappearance of Jim Coutts and Richard O'Hagan signifies a deeper emphasis on politics unabashed, and concern for the next election. Interpolated with the dreamy preoccupations that Trudeau personally favours, it all makes a very strange mix up there at the centre of things in the Langevin Block offices.

Direct Democracy
Trudeau believed he was creating a modern, efficient centre of government power, by-passing the unwieldy public service and centred in himself. He entertained the fantasy of a direct "dialogue" with people, the Canadian people at large.

There were, and are, direct polling techniques as well as attempts through Statistics Canada to take our pulse and learn our state of health – the computerized results to lead to flawless decisions and beneficent laws.

Trudeau once arranged, in those first honeymoon months, to have MPs in to lunch, and to invite to small informal meetings ten or more people from hither and yon – representative Canadians. John Meisel of Queen's University commented that people he knew came away from such sessions reporting an atmosphere too constrained to be fruitful, though they may have given Trudeau a sense of "exploring the options." The gatherings were soon abandoned.

A major attempt at direct democracy was the setting up of Regional Desks at the PMO. The staff manning the Desks were supposed to develop meaningful links of communication with the public, seeking out independent contacts with the academic world, local government officials, and other special interest groups.

It didn't work out. The lines into the Regional Desks got clogged with party-political calls – making Liberal officials and backbench Liberal MPs angry and jealous: eventually the Desks were curtailed. Late in 1975 the new principal secretary, Jim Coutts, fired several of the remaining Desk operators.

The Liberal party strove mightily for a place in the new order. Surely *they* were the grass roots contact Trudeau needed. But even by June 1969 Richard Stanbury, president of the party, was writing, "The feeling of inaccessibility caused by physical limitations has been ameliorated to some extent but there is still an impression that the Prime Minister is protected too much by his staff." He expressed fear that the PMO might "undercut the Party organization and the Members of Parliament as the principal channels of communication between the people and the government."

The party had beefed up its new downtown office on Bank Street. From the time Keith Davey became National Director in 1961 there had been an effort to revitalize the organization. Policy conferences and committees had been set up, and there had been a change in the constitution in 1966 to require the leader of the party to be accountable to the party membership concerning the policy decisions taken at conventions.

Trudeau was quite happy to have the party take over fund-raising – it was on his instructions that the party's Finance Committee with full reponsibility was created. No doubt it left him free for more philosophical pursuits. But he was by no means as willing to let them move in on policy-making.

Provincial advisory groups ("Troikas") were set up to feed party opinion into the Cabinet, and an enlarged "Political Cabinet" was occasionally called to bring top party people into Cabinet discussions. Liberals begging for access were quick to point out that Pearson had lost elections when he listened to academics and civil servants and forgot the politicians. But within a year they were aware that the same thing was happening under Trudeau. The downtown party office got no priority in information from the PMO; instead party people spent a lot of their time trying to get through the barriers to the East Block.

"Co-operation," said President Stanbury, "has not been forthcoming . . . we have not yet succeeded in organizing Cabinet for political purposes . . . there are signs of the Cabinet backsliding . . . "

Stanbury had envisioned the "new" Liberal party as a vehicle for participatory democracy. So what added righteous indignation to his feeling of neglect was his conviction that the party had achieved a new rapport with "the people" and was equipped to serve as the messenger of down-to-earth news to the Prime Minister and Cabinet. Alas, it was not to be.

A massive party convention in 1970, the culmination of two years' preparation, fell flat when Trudeau made it clear that he would not consider himself bound by the delegates' decisions, which included freer abortion laws and a guaranteed annual income among other matters.

After 1970, interest waned. Academics asked to contribute to "thinkers' conferences" for the party saw little evidence of their effect on public affairs, and some believed such political involvement lost them points in the academic world.

When a Cabinet study group looked back at "participation" in September 1970, it rejected any sharing of authority on policy matters with the party. It would be ridiculous to imagine that the party could require the Cabinet to "adhere to policy proposals which may be contrary to their judgment and personal conviction," the study group said bluntly.

In 1975 Toronto left-wing Liberal Stephen Clarkson sent a pessimistic letter to Senator Richard Stanbury. What had been gained from that 1968 upsurge of democracy? It was a question many other 1968-style Liberals who had brought Trudeau to power were also asking.

The Liberal party moved comfortably back into its old ways, meaning power by local patronage.

When Trudeau was touring Lac Megantic, Quebec, in May 1973, a girl in a group of youthful applauders told a reporter: "Our Opportunity for Youth project was cancelled this year and one of the Liberal organizers told us that if we got 300 people out to see Mr. Trudeau this afternoon we'd get our project reinstated next Tuesday."

Though Trudeau had condemned the flagrant patronage system of the bad old Liberals, he had not been four years in office when the administration became notorious for the numbers of defeated Liberal candidates and other party men who were given appointments to the civil service and to various boards and commissions, as well as to the Senate. In March, 1972, David Lewis, leader of the NDP, was telling Trudeau that his performance had "equalled or surpassed every pork-barrelling Prime Minister in the country's history."

While defeated Liberal candidates got a nice choice of jobs on the public payroll, successful Liberal Members of Parliament were kept on their toes, and faithful, with the prospect of becoming a Parliamentary Secretary (a species that proliferated rapidly) with a $5,300-a-year salary bonus. Trudeau has the sole authority to confer these appointments, and he adroitly changes the list every couple of years, just to keep everybody awake and anxious.

With such a rewards system in full swing, the Liberal party scarcely mourns the loss of the rejuvenating spirit which would have returned them to the grass roots. And this avenue of participatory democracy is effectively closed.

The oversized Prime Minister's Office and Privy Council Office are the nation's power centre, secretive, feared and detested by the departmental public service, and in no sense a fresh channel of communication with the people, as Trudeau originally promised.

Pierre Trudeau was never a democrat. The power-encumbered executive that he created (which has not speeded government action: quite the reverse) has perhaps permanently distorted our traditional Parliamentary and administrative forms of government.

And who now even remembers there was once that crazy promise of instant approach to the Prime Minister from us outside? And that his picked group of clever, closeted people would gauge the public will by direct electronic readings and analysis?

How could it work? To feed in the views of citizens to that kind of tight, mechanized operation is about as likely a procedure as letting the members of the Anti-Noise Association come in and help direct approaching aircraft at the Malton control tower.

If *that* was participatory democracy, it deserved a swift burial.

3   The Ramparts

Spreading through Ottawa and in federal offices throughout the land is the vast army of the public service, now numbering almost a quarter of a million people.

There are two major misconceptions about the public service.

One is that it merely administers what is decided elsewhere.

The second is that it is a stable, non-partisan, comfortably dependable force that represents the state, while mere parties come and go.

While these two false notions produce a kind of government by hallucination, there are also new factors present, new practices imposed, which destroy morale and lead to an uncommon degree of neurosis in the ranks of the Ottawa army.

These misconceptions and this state of jitters make it very difficult indeed to *relate* to our government. There can only be anguished resistance to any attempts to establish contact, until some of these distortions are made straight.

Two Myths
There is first, then, the question of who makes the decisions. The problem here is not nearly so much that public servants are making decisions. The problem is the extraordinary tensions produced by public servants either, at the bottom, virtuously refusing to decide on anything, and passing it up the

line, or, at higher levels, arbitrarily taking command, on the strength of their own assessment of what the situation requires and in the full confidence of their anonymity. Public servants, you see, aren't supposed to be blamed for anything. It's in the holy annals of our British inheritance. The public service is faceless and exceedingly faithful, and the minister up top has to answer for anything that goes awry in his department. That puts the civil servant safely out of reach, and becomes a fatal flaw in the whole apparatus, once the function of the public service begins to change.

After the Second World War the federal government came around to the idea that more planning had to be done, to co-ordinate and direct all the new economic and social programs it had started. So who was going to have time to sit and plan? Obviously, the civil servant, who did a lot of sitting anyway. The politician was on his feet and on the move too much; maybe he could be contemplative for two minutes in the bathroom every morning, but no more.

Take a look at the fat Government of Canada Ottawa phone book. Within the departments there are sections for "program"; and then there are other sections called "research," "development," "planning and development," "methodology and structural forecasting," "systems research and development," "planning and evaluation," and any number of other office titles that shield groups of high-priced help busy with figures and plans and briefs. These public servants are not administering anything. They are producing, on order, the raw stuff of new programs and adaptations of old ones. In due course the various papers will be assembled and a single document written. Unfortunately, the planning document has to be written by a ranking public servant who was hired as an administrator, and he is trying to administer and plan at the same time, and he doesn't want to change too much from the ways things are running now. So he makes the new proposals only marginally new. And up goes the document through other prudent hands to the Minister, who will take it to Cabinet.

Michael Pitfield calls it *activism*. He says, " . . . like it or not, over the past couple of decades government has passed decisively from a reactive to an activist mode and this has required and will continue to require far more fundamental changes in what we do and how we do it than have yet been generally realized."

Ottawa Journal, Saturday, Nov. 8, 1975. (Ron Clingen): – A panel of Liberals at the party's convention Friday agreed that bureaucrats in government have too much power and that members of Parliament should be given a greater role in actual policy-making.

In fact, Liberal M.P. Herb Gray insisted, governing party M.P.'s have nowhere near the influence the mandarins do on decisions of cabinet ministers.

Mr. Gray, who was dumped as consumer and corporate affairs minister in the Trudeau cabinet in August, 1974, argued the input of government policy and its application comes more from the public service than from any other source.

"The theory is, of course, that the elected politician gives policy and adminstrative direction to the career civil service which, rather than making policy, carries it out," Mr. Gray noted.

But, he countered, the reality is somewhat different.

"The politicians are mere helpless victims, weak sisters," a bureaucrat told me recently.

Back in the days when General Pearkes was minister of defence, I was into the recreation training program of the RCAF. We developed those 5BX plans and so on – had a program going for the airmen's families at the base as well.

We held a display at an exhibition in Washington and one smart-ass reporter wrote a piece asking why Pearkes was spending thousands of dollars on that kind of thing, when we weren't likely to get RCAF recruits in Washington. Well Pearkes got concerned and issued a statement saying he was going to shut us down. Everything came to a halt.

You see there was some internecine strife, some of the old-line bureaucrats didn't like the size of the budget we were getting. That's usually the way it starts, slicing up the budget. So what I did was get in touch with the Ontario department that was using a lot of our material, – we had thirty-nine publications out, on community development and so on, – and I got the head of that department to write to Pearkes protesting the move to shut us down.

Now of course what happens is that the letter comes down the line from Pearkes' office for *me* to draft an answer. And I wrote a letter about the importance of our program, and how there was no intention of discontinuing it – maybe cutting out a few frills around the edges – and I sent it back up to Pearkes. And Pearkes looked at it and decided he must have been hasty – he had no time to go into it – and signed the letter. So I got copies made of his signed letter and circulated them to my colleagues – that's common practice – and all systems were GO once more.

That's the dynamics of the thing.

Add the considered opinion of Dr. J.E. Hodgetts, academic extraordinary, in a 1973 tome called, "The Canadian Public Service: A Physiology of Government." He says:

We have barely probed the surface of the fundamental issue of bureaucratic accountability, in an era when the balance of effective power tends more and more to be tipped in favour of the submerged part of the governmental iceberg that constitutes the permanent administrative branch.

If you're fussy about such things, consider also that there's no constitutional guide to where the civil service fits in. Hodgetts tells us: "The constitution has nothing to say about the public service. No one is sure whether it is the servant of the cabinet or the legislature."

And he speaks, with stern sadness, of the hierarchical form of the civil service and its chain of command:

. . . the man vested by his place in the hierarchy with the authority to decide may not in fact be capable of making a decision. Indeed, for many of the complex issues now confronting bureaucracies, there may not be a single position in the hierarchy capable of rendering a decision . . .

Walter Rudnicki, a public servant of whom much more later, had reflected on this and he gave me a paper of his to read, which came to the same sorrowful conclusion:

A fundamental deficiency of most government institutional forms is the hierarchical structure. (The file clerk speaks only to the supervisor, the supervisor reports to the Division Chief, who has access to the Branch Director . . .) Policy formulation is, by default, in the hands of a few of the senior administrators of a given department. Burdened as they are with administrative tasks, and encumbered as they may be by vested interest, they have little time or capacity for reflection. Their rise in the system depended, in the main, on administrative and technical competence rather than conceptual capacity. Even if relieved of the pressure of administrative duty, most would be incompetent to formulate and elucidate detailed policies which are coherent with the detailed policies of their sister departments and with the general policies laid down by Parliament. The information which senior officials receive has usually filtered up through so many layers of the stratified department that the policy-making process is often no more complex than simple positive or negative response to exigency.

As they struggle with their acknowledged or unacknowledged inadequacies as power brokers, the public service does not lack for advice. In fact, firm advice on this very subject was recently prepared for them by that little nest of big brains, the Economic Council of Canada. Five years ago, still in the sunrise glow of Trudeau's first term, the Council produced a report called, "Design for Decision-Making." Oddly, this Report had a very limited circulation. I wrestled one out of the Council's library files.

It is directed to the bureaucracy. It advocates the techniques of systematic analysis. It presents a "framework for government decision-making."

The core of the Report is a very simple chart.

Decisions are made on three levels, but each decision flows through a pipeline to the level just below.

On the top level, decisions are made about "policy

objectives." As the text explains, these are big, grand things like keeping our nation healthy and spreading employment evenly from sea to sea. And the decisions are derived from various "priority alternatives" proceeding from an input of "goal indicators," which are arrived at statistically and which show our national state of health and well-being. In the text, one proposed unit in the health goal indicator is the "bed-disability-free day."

The big, national choices are made in the light of such indicators.

Then down the line. At the middle level there is analysis (of the overall objective) – setting up alternatives – and from these alternatives further decisions on *strategies.*

The Report sets down as a good example of "alternative strategies": *either* an increase in welfare *or* an increase in manpower training. (The grand objective here is to reduce poverty.)

At this point I back off and ask you: If you are talking about an unemployed fellow, capable of learning something useful instead of sitting around feeling poor, what brilliant analysis is needed to decide it's better to pay him to learn something than merely to pay him? If on the other hand you're talking about an old lady in a wheel chair, does it take long to decide to pay her welfare instead of sending her on a welding course? Welfare we need and manpower training we need, but they do not seem to me to be alternatives.

But enough of such subjective irrelevance. On to the third and bottom level of the decision-making chart.

Down the pipeline flows the strategy decision to enter into a choice of programs (sometimes called "tactics"). It is recommended here to set up experimental models, demonstration programs, to aid in the final decision about which government program ought ultimately to go into operation.

And that's the bottom line.

Except that there's a little encircling channel of communication called "feedback" running from the program back up to the other levels. The Report says this aspect often gets neglected, and the people carrying out the programs fail to report on how well they're doing, which might have a substantive effect on new "strategies" or even on new "policy objectives."

(The Cabinet meets. Michael Pitfield is there. *Maybe it's bet-ter not to train these guys? Maybe maximum relief from poverty should be dumped? Who's for MILITARY training? Or a moon colony? THINK, chaps, THINK.*)

The appalling thing about the chart is that it's a closed circuit. The writers of the Report injected a pious concern that all the decisions not be made at one national centre. But with such a system (Pitfield's "total system"!) there is no other pos-sibility. How many centres of power can the country have, each sustained by a battery of statisticians providing goal indi-cators, and sizable field battalions trying out experimental programs? Centralization, tightly centralized control, is inher-ent in this decision-making chart.

And what room, I politely ask, for the chance "input" of a mere participating democratic citizen at large?

What room for Parliament?

The Report came out in the fall of 1971. It would be nice to dismiss it as one of the excesses inspired by Trudeau's first "new style" administration. But the writers noted that some training in new-style decision-making was underway at that date. A footnote said: "One aspect of the processes of policy-making is being covered at the federal level by a training course for analysts in key policy-advisory units of government." And we can't ignore evidence that the concepts are still at work, as in the Cabinet's seasonal "priorities exercise," and the mandatory preparation of two, not one, pol-icy proposals, as "alternatives" to the Cabinet committees. Then we have Sylvia Ostry saying, albeit wistfully, that she believes we must continue the admittedly difficult task of de-veloping "social indicators." Sylvia Ostry is now deputy minis-ter of the Department of Consumer and Corporate Affairs, before that head of Statistics Canada, and before that, in 1971 when the Report was written, director of the Economic Coun-cil of Canada.

What we have in 1976 is a group of top advisers and bu-reaucrats trying to govern by such mechanistic models of efficiency, defensive and secretive by now, but not yet giving in to the inevitable weight of the encumbrances they have as-sumed.

Prime Minister Trudeau is, unfortunately for him, the king-piece. And the model undoubtedly appeals to him personally, since it leaves him room to lead the cerebral adventures up top. But, as Barry Callaghan prophesied in 1968, he also tries to be pragmatic, and the two things don't fit. Sometimes he bursts out without warning, causing pain and consternation, as when he decides he will impose a three-year program of wage and price controls. When he does such things he conveys a sense of the heroic, befitting a man who has just punched his way out of a cocoon.

One of the reasons why "Design for Decision-Making" was published without fanfare, is that the writers examined some sectors of the federal government that had attempted to introduce these patterns and they came down very hard on Manpower Training. What they saw was such an obvious failure that only the most determined theorists could persist, in the face of it, to present their Report in good faith.

The Department of Manpower and Immigration had set up, when it was established in 1966, a major division called the Program Development Service, headed by an assistant deputy minister, and dedicated to systematic evaluation and research – "far in advance of the activities in many of the older federal departments, although some changes in this direction are certainly under way," says the Report.

The grand "objective" was economic growth. (Not, be it noted, "reduction of poverty" as in the example quoted earlier.) Manpower Training was a "strategy," part of the effort to have a work force available, trained in the right skills to keep industry humming.

There may be questioning now about economic growth as desirable, but there wasn't in 1966, or in 1970. When Allan MacEachen was Minister he reiterated firmly, before a 1970 Standing Committee of the House of Commons: "The main objective of the Department is to further the economic growth of Canada by endeavouring to ensure that the supply of manpower matches the demand qualitatively, quantitatively and geographically."

Well, the Report spotted one flaw in the operation right away. The government had persisted for five years in training people in classrooms, despite a great deal of evidence that you get better results when you train them on the job, in an industrial setting. What were all those trainees doing at school desks instead of on the factory floor?

The next strange thing it observed was that 40 per cent of the enrollees were being trained to make up gaps in their basic education: receiving courses approximately at a secondary school level. The courses were called "Upgrading Skills." The reason the trainees were in classrooms, picking up what they hadn't got earlier in the public school system, was because there was no crying need for skilled men and industrial employers had no interest in participating in the scheme.

Whereupon the Report commented: "In a period of high unemployment, when few skill vacancies are apparent and when training for particular occupational skills is therefore hazardous, there exists the possibility that such basic training may be used, as it were, simply as an absorbent."

So there you are. If they had followed through on their technocratic model, the "objectives" of the Manpower Department would immediately have been switched to "absorbing surplus workers." Almost a billion and a half dollars had been spent in five years on "manpower training," but what had developed had been a simple response to unemployment, a subsidized school program to keep young people busy learning something. Private industry didn't want the bother and expense of training people "on the job" for non-existent positions. There weren't sufficient numbers of unfilled vacancies in *any* skills to justify the program.

So what was the evaluation section of the Department doing? It was trying to figure out how to measure whether a young man's chance of employment was "better" or "unchanged" after a training course. (The methods of measurement didn't stand up, the Report observed sternly.) It was trying to decide whether the costs equalled the benefits to the government and the country. The Report states, " . . . when account is taken of the work experience of trainees for several years prior to training, the program does not appear to have resulted in improvement in employment." This despite Manpower claims that benefits were on the order of two to three dollars for each dollar of expenditure! Somebody was messing up the figures. What possible motive could have been at work?

None of this discouraged the Economic Council. More information was needed. More analysis. More feedback. The perfect decision-making system is there somewhere: we must press on.

If you want to pursue the horror story of the Manpower Department, wander through the halls in the large Bourque Building on Rideau Street. The Strategic Planning and Research Division. The Research Projects Group with constituents called Home Base "A," Home Base "B" and other Home Bases up to "G." Don't ask what people are doing behind those doors. You're happier not knowing.

There is an awful innocence about this approach to guiding the public affairs of the country. A fantasy is created, a pure model. Living, breathing people try to conform to phantom images. Once set in motion, who dares call a halt, who dares point out that the Emperor has no clothes?

What has brought the public service to this state of affairs is the assumption of the policy-making role, without discarding the belief that public servants work in secret, the anonymous behind-the-scenes support of duly elected political masters, with *no right* to consult the outside word. Hence the closed circuit of decision-making.

Certainly there are critics who would like to reverse the process, and leave the civil service with a minor role in policy-making. One who has become explosive on the subject is Professor Douglas Hartle, once with the Treasury Board, who in 1975 told the Canadian Institute of Public Administration bluntly:

> In a parliamentary system, the bureaucrat should have relatively little decision-making discretion . . . Any Minister who delegates substantial powers to a senior official, who in turn delegates some of these powers to his subordinates, who in turn delegates, *ad infinitum,* is a fool if he does not specify the ground rules under which they are to proceed. He is, if he does not set forth such rules, inviting political insensitivity at best and old-fashioned corruption at worst.

Political insensitivity. That means insensitivity to us.

One of the more curious inversions of meaning attached to the much-abused word "political" occurs on the lips of the civil servant. "Political" is a sneer-word. It is some human consideration that gets in the way of his pure, detached, scientific decision on the way things ought to be done.

The myth that the civil service does not make policy is as false as the second myth, that the civil service is stoically non-partisan amid the moving seas of politics, the firm rock on which our institutions rest.

This myth is perpetuated by people like Dr. Gordon Smith, who is head of a sub-section of the Privy Council called "Machinery of Government." Speaking before a Parliamentary Committee he drew attention to the superiority of our system because "public servants in Canada are appointed through the merit system" and he would not recommend any move to "politicize the public service."

Scarcely an eyebrow was raised, however, when Jack Pickersgill was reported to have told an Ottawa meeting (in May 1972) that public servants have an obligation to support the party in power, and cannot be neutral when dealing with the Opposition. A director of information told me that when Opposition Members come to him for information, he considers it his duty to let his Minister know about it. The sense of loyalty to the Liberals pervades Ottawa. And in general elections civil servants trot obediently to the polls to attest their loyalty: the four city ridings of Ottawa East, Ottawa West, Ottawa Centre and Ottawa-Carleton voted Liberal in 1974 as they have almost without exception for decades past. A by-election in Ottawa-Carleton in late 1976 shattered this serene state of affairs. (It appeared to be a protest against the language training program.)

At the Berger Commission inquiry in Yellowknife in April 1976, Douglas Stephen, a regional director of the Canadian Wildlife Service, testified that he had not prosecuted some companies under environmental protection regulations because of the political consequences such prosecutions might bring. He added that he felt it was his duty to put "wings and a halo" on his Minister, Jean Marchand.

Many such civil servants are comfortably and openly Liberal. The distinction fades between them and the special group of "political appointments," the "aides" of the Cabinet Ministers. The number of aides has grown wildly. Before Trudeau's time there were only a few; now almost every Minister has several, to a total of nearly one hundred, outside the staff of the Prime Minister. These people work frankly on party matters; among them are a number of defeated Liberal candidates. Their influence spreads throughout the public servic.

Between the bureaucracy and the Liberal party, writes columnist Richard Gwyn: "the less tangible ties are the more important ones. An identity of thought and behaviour has developed, and is intensifying."

At the beginning of the Sky Shops Affair, attention focused briefly on an exchange of memos between two "aides": Carmel Carriere, executive secretary to Jean Marchand, and Andy Chatwood, executive assistant to Don Jamieson. The memos, written in 1971, seemed to lead to a reversal of a Cabinet decision to open up the Sky Shops lease for tender. The fresh decision, to extend the lease, led to charges being laid against Liberal Senator Louis Giguere and others. But what part did mere "aides" play in this transaction? What other public servants are implicitly involved, in the course of their jobs, in what are essentially party machinations?

Yet the myth of the Civil Servant Incorruptible is still there. Trudeau himself vacillates between the myth and the reality. At a full-dress occasion at Government House in 1974 to honour retiring Undersecretary of State for External Affairs Edgar Ritchie, Mr. Trudeau described our public servants as "the symbol of permanence in the state, the guarantor of the continuity of society, which, whatever the winds of change, must be respected and preserved according to the letter and spirit of the law."

But it was Mr. Trudeau who, when increasing the research staff for Opposition parties in parliament, explained that the poor blighters needed this support because "*we* have the civil service."

If all this makes the civil servant seem a spineless chap, consider the various devices that surround him with a Big Brother atmosphere.

These men and women are locked into a competitive work place that makes General Motors look like a round table of brotherly love. To succeed they must climb, within rigid rules and classifications. They must put their careers, and the scheming and the time necessary to advance their careers, ahead of mere attention to duty.

When I was a candidate in an Ottawa riding in the last federal election, a civil servant wound up a long, regretful discourse by saying to me, "Everything about the classification system they use reinforces *status*. It forces competition and alienation at every level."

Let me quote again from something Walter Rudnicki wrote, a paper given to a Community Development Conference of social workers in 1974, on the workings of bureaucracy:

> . . . it is not unusual to observe people who spend their days worrying about whether their superior likes them or whether they will get a promotion. Others may be resentful or angry that some expected reward did not materialize, or that it went to the wrong person. It (the civil service office) is often a place of conflict, anxiety and suspicion . . . Successful behaviour tends to become a series of complexly determined manoeuvers which have little relevance to the job that one is supposed to do or, indeed, to the people one is supposed to serve.

> Let us imagine a young man or woman, fresh out of university, bright-eyed, creative, optimistic and ready to perform great deeds. Let us assume that the organization that has just hired the new graduate exists for the ostensible purpose of serving some sector of the public or a particular client group. It usually takes as long as a year, but by then, the new employee realizes that so much psychic and emotional energy has to be expended in succeeding within a bureaucracy that little is left over to invest in the public. The impact on human behaviour of paternalistic relationships,

takes the form in many people of a rapid erosion in motivation, creativity and interest. Reality becomes the inter-office memorandum – and success the acquisition of another status symbol.

Just as poignantly J. E. Hodgetts wrote, in his 1973 book called *The Canadian Public Service,* of the work environment:

> . . . the powerful play of personalities in ubiquitous committees; the personal whirlpools of power and influence; the day-to-day drain on the psyche from living in a pyramided beehive; the struggle to achieve status, a self-respecting career, the recognition of one's peers in a formal hierarchy wedded to anonymity; the blunting of initiative and the tamping down of ambition that comes when a project is thwarted or disappears up the line into silence; the imbalance of a highly formalized system of work distribution that leaves a few at the top with too much to do while many are never afforded a chance to realize their full potential . . .

The symbols of achievement are the most crass one can imagine. So many more square inches of office room and window space. A bigger desk, with a top of walnut rather than plastic veneer is the reward for breaking into the executive, SX1, class. An SX2 gets free parking. All this solemnly laid down and rigidly followed. One of the dreariest little stories I heard around Ottawa was of a young fellow who decided to take *his own rug* to the office to cover a bare floor. His position did not entitle him to a rug, and he had, in much humility, to cart it home again.

It's a monumental paradox, but in fact the ultimate folly of the private enterprise concept shows up in our public service. The concept is that a vigorous pursuit of personal rewards produces the common good. This assumption animates the bureaucratic structure; it has become more virulent during the Trudeau years with greater emphasis on the managerial skills and techniques borrowed from business practice. As each person scratches for his or her own betterment, the huge organization flounders in a mire of inefficiency.

So why do public servants not speak out against conditions in their workplace?

Because it is forbidden. Not in any law, and yet enforced by law. Professor Kenneth Kernaghan at the request of the Institute of Public Administration recently tried to set down the mode of conduct considered proper for the civil servant in regard to "public comment." Among the things Kernaghan thought a public servant should observe were: "to restrict criticism of policies and their administration to the confines of his department or agency and communicate his personal views through departmental or agency channels," and "express his views with moderation when making any public comment, even if he has authorization or is on leave of absence."

In June 1975, an administrative officer working for the Department of Supply and Services, Arthur Stewart, wrote an article for the Ottawa *Citizen* criticizing the "empire-building" going on in that Department and stating that the employees there were disgruntled and disillusioned, a state of affairs that "must be laid directly at Mr. Goyer's doorstep." Jean-Pierre Goyer was the Minister. Stewart defended his action on the grounds that he is president of the union local in that Department, and felt he had a right and a duty to challenge the employer in the situation. The Department thought otherwise. Stewart was suspended for three months by the deputy minister, with a loss of pay of about $6,500. His lawyer, after the grievance hearing, called that "a really crushing fine for a mild criticism," and urged, "It is time to upset that foolish tradition that muzzles public servants." Foolish or not, the action against Stewart was sustained, with a reduced penalty. It's not exactly surprising that no other public servants rushed into print to defend Stewart or to challenge the traditional "muzzling."

Public servants take an Oath of Office and Secrecy, worded to sound very tough, yet of uncertain validity. An employee can be reprimanded for breaking the Oath, but there are no prescribed penalties. Action is up to the supervising officers.

Then there's the security clearance system, which means investigation by the Royal Canadian Mounted Police. Civil servants don't talk about these investigations into their private lives: many of them don't know they're the subject of files tucked away in RCMP drawers. Others, who have had a difficult time getting responsible positions because of suspicions about their past, refuse to comment. "My case isn't typical," one such man told me. "I don't think you could generalize from it so I'd rather not discuss it."

Security clearance is required of every public servant who is considered to have access to "classified" information, and the extension of this classification system to all sorts of documents having nothing to do with national security means that a very large group of public servants must be screened. Police files are searched for subversive or criminal records in such cases and, when the public servant is to have access to "secret" or "top secret" classifications, the RCMP does a "background" investigation of the individual. Only on the basis of the RCMP report is security clearance granted.

For any of a number of very special reasons, a public servant may in fact be blacklisted, and may find himself unaccountably sidetracked to a deadend job or, if he rashly resigns, unable to get a new position at Ottawa.

Public servants are sometimes required to attend special RCMP briefings. For example, a film showing native people suspected of "violent" attitudes toward society was part of a warning against association with "certain groups."

"We're all getting paranoid," a woman told me after attending such a briefing.

One of the least attractive additions to Parliament Hill, that postcard riot of red tulips, green lawn and heaven-pointing Peace Tower, is the installation of three powerful telescopic cameras set in strategic rooftop locations to record things for the police. They were first noticed by reporters the day after the very large (and very peaceful) picketing on Parliament Hill by trade unions protesting wage and price controls in March 1976. Other reporters had remarked that the demonstration seemed to get very little support from the public service unions; only a handful joined the march.

If electronic surveillance makes him nervous, the public servant may also find himself frustrated and helpless when his career advancement depends on such dubious machinery as the "Data Stream," a constant annoyance to people who dispute the wisdom of the computer in selecting which employees should be considered for which jobs. "If you appeal the decision you're a pariah," a professional civil servant told me.

One of the worst intrusions into the public servant's life during the recent years of intense second-language training has been the preparing of linguistic profiles of staff in every department. The profile records not only the proficiency of the employee in English and French, but a "willingness indicator" which is the unit head's assessment of how much enthusiasm the employee is exhibiting toward the bilingualism program.

And meanwhile other surveys are delving into the state of happiness of the nation's employees. The Department of Industry, Trade and Commerce embarked on a survey of the 2,-500 members of its staff in late 1975. Partial results revealed an unusual degree of discontent, lassitude and anxiety. One of the prescriptions from the survey research group was for an extra hour at lunchtime when the employee might go for a dip in a swimming pool.

Input – Output, Citizenwise

Which all adds up to a work environment not conducive to frank good fellowship. It's probably remarkable that so many public servants stay human, and remain on reasonably good terms with humanity "outside."

Sometimes, mind you, it's as awkward as meeting people from Mars.

One of the greatest feats of non-involvement of citizens was accomplished by the Habitat people before the big United Nations Conference on Human Settlements in Vancouver in June 1976. A budget of something less than a million dollars was appropriated for a secretariat in the Urban Affairs Department. That would cover Canada's duties as host to the Conference, plus our efforts to participate in the event.

A group of sixteen people were to drum up business on the "participation" side. Their method was to slip unobtrusively from town to town, inserting a boxed ad in formal type in the local newspapers. Sometimes they got as many as twenty people at one meeting.

At a conference of women from volunteer organizations in November 1975, a harassed, very nervous young person from

61

Habitat attempted with blackboard charts and acronyms to explain the *participation thrust:* she was halfway through before she realized that this naïve audience didn't even savvy that NGO means Non-Government Organization.

It was a dismal interchange. After that sort of preparation, even the bright magnetism of British peeress Barbara Ward couldn't interest Canada much in "Habitat."

Information from the civil service to the people is a major subject in itself, so let's leave it for the next chapter.

There is however the matter of body contact. There are occasions in the course of his duties when a public servant does meet a non-public servant eyeball to eyeball.

What inspires the public servant in these encounters is generally described as the "adversary system."

There is a smart-ass attitude in pre-conference sessions by public servants. They're trying to anticipate the enemy's position, outwit, outsmart and outmanoeuvre him. They draw up a "game plan" for the occasion. They get a very exciting sense of being *in,* where the power lies.

Their objective is to prevent any meaningful influence on their activities by the public they are employed to serve.

The adversary system has sharpened since Trudeau came to power with his promise of participatory democracy. The "client" groups – like the native people – are actually funded to permit them to draw up positions from which to confront *government* positions. It's not even-handed justice. The dribble of researchers and legal services thus made available to the "client" is massively outweighed by the department (plus Privy Council) with which he must deal.

Does anyone ask who the *government* officials are supposed to be representing in these negotiations? Is it the State, and the State's treasury, protecting itself from assault by a too-demanding minor segment of the nation's people? That's a small part of it really, and slicing the pie is a process that any group can accept, if explanations are clear and just.

No, public servants on such occasions too often fight for less legitimate ends, such as acclaim for their Ministers and the Liberal party from the taxpayers who are presumed to applaud evidence of restraint in spending.

Or, sometimes, simply, they fight to defend their own comfortable positions and their own settled way of doing things. Usually it is a government plan, drawn up within the bureaucracy, that is placed before such meetings, and the bureaucracy closes ranks to defend it valiantly. Proposals from the "other side" are taken away from the meeting to be chewed up and declared impracticable.

As well as funding adversary groups, the bizarre idea has been raised to provide the public with "advocates," from within the bureaucracy itself. Advocates have been seriously considered by the Department of Consumer Affairs, which compromised by funding "advocates" on behalf of us poor exploited consumers within a satellite organization (funded by government), the Consumer Association of Canada. The idea is also being put forward in the Woman's Program area of the Secretary of State Department – to help women's organizations lobby the government.

It's at least an indication that some public servants have twinges of conscience about the uneven battles between the bureaucracy and the ordinary citizen.

Accused of alienating the citizenry, the government has sometimes responded by promising to decentralize its operations, to establish a federal presence in the hinterlands. Alex Campbell, Prince Edward Island Premier, is one critic who says bluntly that the federal government might as well stay in Ottawa, for all the good it's doing in Summerside. "They don't come down here to create an important interface, they have no clear mandate to seek local involvement. They often go through the appearance of consultation, when their plans are already formed," he complained.

The Bureaucrat-Entrepreneur
When the Trudeau government took office it tried one major tactic to rectify the entrenched nature of the public service. It decided to ventilate the upper strata by making it easy and attractive for executives from private business to take government posts, at least for short periods in their careers.

It's been a strange experiment, doing much more harm than good.

The public service has been reared in an atmosphere that insists that government performance is inferior to private business, which has "know-how," and "initiative," and "gets things done." So the bureaucracy rather humbly accepted the newcomers and set about learning from them.

The first effect was a vast increase in the upper ranks, not all, of course, from private business, but as a direct result of Trudeau's concern for "management." From 1970 to 1975 public service employment increased by 26 per cent. But in the same period the executive class grew by 82 per cent. The select group including deputy ministers are in a salary bracket with a top figure of $60,000 a year.

To advise the government on how to do right by its executives, a committee from the private sector was set up, first under J. V. Clyne and now under Allen Lambert.

The transformation of government offices from drab to resplendent has had considerable documentation by cynical news gatherers. This again reflects the need to ape private industry, where the executive suite, replete with bar and lounge and luxury, is now the norm.

To reassure the public while making appointments from the private sector, like William Teron plucked from the role of private developer to head the Central Mortgage and Housing Corporation (CMHC), Mr. Trudeau introduced conflict-of-interest guidelines in 1973. Deputy ministers and others of high rank are supposed to divest themselves of connections with business that might give them a pecuniary interest in any government transaction. They do this by putting their corporation holdings into "blind" or "frozen" trusts. Naturally suspicion hovers over the capital: do these devices sufficiently divorce the public servant from his former private enterprise, to which he may in fact return? Doesn't he ever feel tempted to sneak a little look at how his trust is being managed? The guidelines are not at all explicit on how he must go about removing himself from the temptation to profit by inside knowledge; they merely require that "Upon appointment to office, public servants are expected to arrange their private affairs in a manner that will prevent conflicts of interest from arising." The public servants have to open their books on request, to show how they've met this requirement. Opposition Members think this isn't enough.

Scandal-ridden Ottawa in the recent past has heard evidence that public servants had lively little businesses going on the side, using their government telephones to head up operations. A number of very lucrative cleaning contracts for government buildings were disclosed. A group of Statistics Canada employees peddled information through their private consulting firm.

We've had enough scandal around Ottawa in the past two years to emphasize the murkiness of relations between private profit and inside privileged positions. How did it happen that such possibilities did not enter Trudeau's head when he first espoused the idea of closer ties between government and business?

The sensational charges of misconduct do possibly less damage than the imposition – in good faith – of absurdly inappropriate business techniques to government. The current foul-up and slowdown of government affairs stems in very large part from the mismanagement introduced by "sound business practices."

I mean such things as Program Planning and Budgeting; Operational Performance Measurement Systems; Management by Objectives; Cost-Benefit Analysis and Cost-Effectiveness Studies, all in vogue at Ottawa during the Trudeau years at great cost and waste and frustration.

I am going to call as witness again economics professor Douglas Hartle, speaking during the proceedings of the Canadian Institute of Public Administration. Here is a bit of what he said:

> There has been a tendency which can be traced back to . . . the Glassco Commission that reported in the mid-sixties, to suppose that the public sector was, in some sense, mismanaged relative to the private sector . . . In my view, the idea that public servants are managers is fallacious. In a well-run system, public servants are not managers: they are policy advisers and/or emissaries (negotiators) and/or administrators . . . The Hoover and Glassco Commissions made a

fundamental error, in my opinion. They were simple-minded in assuming that the techniques and processes that have proven useful in the private sector could be applied, virtually without modification, to the public sector . . .

In the public sector there is no equivalent to a profit and loss statement. The record of assets and liabilities is virtually meaningless . . .

Spending agencies do not take seriously the requests for estimates of their future expenditures (PPB). They simply extrapolate the next year's requests at a constant rate. Why should they bother to do otherwise when the numbers are not taken seriously by those responsible for putting together the budget for the coming year . . . ?

It was naïve to assume that agreement could be reached as to *the* objective of each program. Most programs have multiple objectives and some of them cannot be admitted . . .

I am highly skeptical about the efficacy of MBO (Management by Objectives). Too often, in my experience, MBO costs more in time and energy than it produces. Endless meetings. Haggling over jurisdictional territory. Drafts and redrafts of statements of objectives to ensure that they are sufficiently vague. No real monitoring of performance against the stated objectives – sometimes because this is impossible and sometimes because it is uncomfortable for the senior officer . . .

Cost-benefit analysis . . . is a technique looked upon by decision makers as a tool in the adversarial process . . . I cannot recall any instance where a cost-benefit study played a decisive role in the decision to proceed with or reject any proposed major federal project . . .

And so on. Hartle served his time as consultant with the Treasury Board. His almost total rejection now of the fancy techniques the government has been playing with for the past several years is still mildly shocking to many public servants. But other critics are coming to the same conclusion.

A department of government is not a boot factory.

The business ethic does not apply.

The idea is not to do business with the public, but to serve them.

The bureaucracy is not the people's antagonist, but an agent entrusted to provide collective goods paid for by the people.

You'd never guess it, in Trudeau's Ottawa.

4 InfoCan and The Right To Know

After Trudeau's 1968 election his first major creation as a visible link between government and people was Information Canada. But InfoCan retreated from its hopeful inauguration with awkward haste. And in December 1975 it was the unlamented first victim of Trudeau's budget-cutting exercise, part of the anti-inflation program. There were other government expenditures that were just as questionable and would have saved the taxpayer more money. But InfoCan had been for five years a large white elephant. No doubt it was also, to Trudeau, an annoying reminder of his first ambitious concept of new-style government. He wielded the axe with relish.

InfoCan had an annual budget of just under $10 million. What exactly did it *do*?

When it was established in April 1970 the Tories thundered that Trudeau had set up "a propaganda machine." This it wasn't. It also failed to perform even the most practical of its terms of reference, as a fast, skilled technical service to improve the delivery of information about government to the public. It decided from the beginning not to touch the established, separate information services of the various departments, who went on doing their own innocuous thing.

It took under its wing the old Queen's Printer bookshops and the old Exhibition Commission – both now shunted to the Department of Supply and Services.

But the saddest part of the failure of InfoCan is that it never even approached what it might have been – a channel of information in and out, a stimulator of discussion and debate and review of government policies and programs. This was only a timid wish advanced by good fairies at InfoCan's birth. No one ever seriously tried to make it happen.

Appearing early on Trudeau's agenda – in fact number one on the earliest "priority" list – was *information*. The Super Group, infatuated with electronics, expressed profound contempt for the dusty bundles of dull dull press releases churned out to explain fisheries, agriculture, defence, welfare and every other kind of program – all of them rolling down a conveyor belt to the wastebaskets of the nation.

So, two months after his election, Trudeau appointed a Task Force on Government Information. It was chaired by d'Iberville Fortier with Bernard Ostry, formerly of the CBC, and Tom Ford, journalist from Winnipeg, as members. They worked with unusual despatch.

The report, when it came out a year later, took as a point of departure "the people's right to know" and stated in its introduction: " . . . the governments of the West have grown terribly out of touch with tens of millions of their people. These people neither believe what their governments say, nor care about them, nor expect much more from them than the right to avoid starvation . . . They are the lost, the unreached . . . In addition to those who are alienated, uncomprehending and discontented, however, there are those who simply feel that their governments do not level with them."

Early in the period while the Task Force was at work, there were intensive discussions of information-dispensing as it related to the holy of holies, the PMO and PCO. A Secretariat on Information was considered as a way of improving things, a body "much like the economic policy and social policy secretariats that already exist." There was wise observation of the need to get *some* information out of the PCO to the public: " . . . the new directives given by the PM concerning the secrecy of information arising out of Cabinet meetings probably calls for some sort of balancing step in order to ensure that someone will be briefing the press on what happens . . . ," a confidential memo said. Newsmen today wish that idea had materialized; it did not.

Cabinet remained mum, and so did the PCO and PMO.

After chewing it over a bit, the PCO people let it be known that they saw it as no part of their duty to inform the media or the public of the high level decisions taken in the inner sanctum. *Any* information at that level had political connotations and must come from the Prime Minister. The Prime Minister, as it happened, undertook to hire press secretaries especially drilled in the purveyance of no information. For several months after the latest of them, Pierre O'Neil, departed in August 1975, the position remained unfilled, and because O'Neil had been required to exercise the most subtle skills of non-communication, the vacancy was scarcely noticed. A revamped triumvirate has now been introduced, under Richard O'Hagan, and could undoubtedly win the confidence and gratitude of the capital's newsmen if it would deliver reliable background briefing. This has never been done during the Trudeau regime and so far there are no signs that it's about to occur.

Tight-lipped at the East Block, the Super Group still, in 1968 and 1969, saw the dispensing of general information from the departments as a high priority. From the first, there had been a semi-developed idea that improved information would fulfil campaign promises of "participatory democracy." This was certainly in Trudeau's mind. The Task Force report when it appeared, used the phrase "participatory democracy" over and over. But it did not come to grips with the idea of reciprocal information, which is surely what participation is all about.

Right there in the Privy Council Office, any attempt to view a government information service as a channel for citizens to talk back to their government, died in its tracks. When Fortier talked to Michael Pitfield and Roméo LeBlanc (Pitfield was secretary to the Priorities and Planning Committee of the Cabinet. LeBlanc, now Minister of Fisheries and Environment, was the PM's Press Secretary.) they rejected the idea, deciding that "a great deal of further exploration will have to be carried out in the area of participatory democracy and the role information may play in it," according to Fortier's memo at that time.

In the Privy Council deliberations, the most brutal comment came from Jim Davey:

It is one thing to talk about the administrative efficiency of the preparation of press releases and government documents, it is entirely another to enter into the field of feedback, of public reaction to government programs or policy and to discuss the notion of participation.

Jim Davey saw information as "a resource as are raw materials, fixed plant, moving plant, and money. It may also be a finished product such as a decision, or passed on as semi-processed . . . Unfortunately, there is only a very rudimentary beginning to the development of an information science." He saw the government "machine" as "largely an information processing operation" with a "very low process efficiency."

The Task Force got as far down the road as the need for people to know what's going on in order that they may participate intelligently. But though vague thoughts were voiced of a two-way street, an intercom that meant the government used its ears as well as its voice, the idea was too large to be tackled. It was only Information Out. No more. Even Information Out didn't progress far.

Among the comments received by the Task Force in the course of preparing its report were two perceptive ones that sought to open up the bigger possibilities. One came from the Canadian Association for Adult Education, that sturdy pioneer of phenomenal "participation" in the early days of "Farm Radio Forum." It argued for an agency (perhaps itself?) to present public issues, using all the appropriate media, to arouse citizen input – before government action.

And Norman Ward, from the Department of Economics and Political Science, University of Saskatchewan, told the Task Force bluntly that he saw little connection between information services from government, and participatory democracy. Citizens must do something positively, not be informed passively. As for "social surveys," they might give the interviewer a sense of participation, but the interviewee merely feels he is being used.

John Meisel of Queen's University came close to the mark when he speculated in a letter to Bernard Ostry:

> The only really effective development that could, I believe, induce people to take a greater interest in political parties and in other mechanisms for 'participatory democracy' would be to give them a sense of genuine participation by making it possible for them to influence decisions made by governments and to see that their activities have, in fact, led to a particular set of government decisions. It is obvious that only if we adopt a greatly more decentralized governmental system would this be possible . . .

On February 19, 1969, the members of the Task Force met with the Prime Minister at 24 Sussex Drive. Present also were Michael Pitfield, Roméo LeBlanc and Jim Davey. The first draft of the Task Force report was discussed. One participant said the Prime Minister's first response was "wild enthusiasm," because "this was one of the first occasions when he had been presented with a report which in some way came to grips with the problem of democratic participation."

But the "wild enthusiasm" died in the careful explanations of his advisers. The group pointed out that the purpose of an information service might be to improve feedback, but at the same time one couldn't lose sight of the fact "that the responsibility for participation in decisions rested very squarely at every moment with the government which was alone responsible, in most cases, for opening up an issue for debate and selecting the moment when this was done."

The meeting favoured a unification and streamlining of government information and only speculated on other possible measures. Social surveys, to get public reaction to legislation and programs already in effect, were favourably considered. The nearest approach to involving the public was a suggestion for Citizen's Advisory Bureaux, a favourite idea of Bernard Ostry's. They would be local offices where news and views might conceivably be exchanged. This recommendation got into the final version of the Task Force report but was left out when the Prime Minister announced in the House the decision to establish Information Canada.

The Task Force report had made seventeen recommendations. Prominent among them was the establishment of a central agency, to be called Information Canada. The role proposed for Information Canada included an oblique reference to feedback from citizens at large:

A prime function of Information Canada would be the fostering of the people's direct and informed participation in federal affairs. It would emphasize relevant research, and develop feedback on federal information from the regions of the country. Its concerns would therefore involve not only the distribution of information but also the government's ability to keep abreast of changing social circumstances and the changing needs of the people.

It was a function that InfoCan was never to carry out.

The creation of the new agency was announced on April 1, 1970. The Opposition parties in the House greeted it with cries of horror. It looked like a "propaganda machine" to them. The entrenched information sections of the departments dug in their heels against losing any of their staff or operations, and it was very quickly determined that all of them could carry on as before. What new functions were to be performed to increase their efficiency was never decided; one project after another was shot down. For example, each department independently acquires sophisticated audio-visual equipment, even though it may frequently be not in use. In the first year of InfoCan's existence, separate information staffs of the various federal departments grew from 900 to 1992 people, and they have been growing ever since.

When Labour Minister Martin O'Connell tabled InfoCan's first report in the House of Commons in March 1972 the Opposition hooted and jeered at the very name. The Conservative party had already gone on record that the agency would be abolished as soon as they had any say in the matter. The press greeted the occasion with hilarity, mostly because the report was a year late, covering the period from April 1970 to April 1971, and because InfoCan had to be informed by newsmen that its report had been tabled in the House that day and could the media have some copies please. Getting the copies to the Press Gallery from IncoCan, three blocks away, took three hours.

A month earlier, someone had leaked a memo from R.J.A. Phillips, deputy director, to Jean-Louis Gagnon, director, saying: "The record of the past six months . . . leads one to conclude that it is urgent to consider some projects to justify our budget and existence."

On his campaign rounds in late September 1972, Trudeau told a questioning reporter in Winnipeg that the reason Information Canada existed was "to point out the lacunae." He left the newsmen to fumble for their dictionaries and make what they could of that reply.

The visible InfoCan was a chain of bookstores in Canada's main cities, the Queen's Printer bookshops of former years. The Ottawa store was designed like a television set with cute raised daises and little carpeted steps, but its stock was outdated and depressing. There you could still buy Hansard for a nickle, but you could not buy, in any shape or form, a simple description of Parliament and its offices and members. For that, one had to apply by mail order to a private dealer, Pierre Normandin, who sells the only standard publication on the subject, *Canadian Parliamentary Guide,* for ten dollars a copy. This time-honoured arrangement goes back to some cobwebby act of patronage, and was left undisturbed by InfoCan.

InfoCan conducted a Citizens' Inquiry Service. The telephone number was listed in the Ottawa phone book under *Government of Canada, Frequently Called Numbers* – twenty-third in an alphabetical list of thirty-five. It was not advertised, though it appeared in a modest brochure (available at the bookstore if you asked for it), called *Information Canada, At Your Service.*

I tried that number one day shortly before InfoCan folded. Hoping to sound like an Average Worried Person, I tried a political question, I asked if the federal government was going to bail out the Olympic Games. A girl with a fresh young voice said she would find out for me, and even volunteered, with a giggle, that she certainly hoped it wasn't. She did get back to me, twice in fact, over the next day and a half. Once to tell me she was going to phone the Olympic Committee in Montreal, and next to deliver their answer. (The answer: As of now, no.) The Inquiry Service was obviously trying. In fact when the whole thing was being disbanded, senior officers at InfoCan cited the Inquiry Service as one of their best and most promising efforts. It was used to a surprising extent, considering its modest and self-effacing nature.

Most inquiries have always been made directly to the departments concerned. Sometimes the departments can be very helpful, as when the Experimental Farm identifies the aphids on your dahlias and tells you how to get rid of them. On other matters you may phone six successive numbers and end up receiving a copy of a speech the Minister made two months ago. Or you may run into touchy areas, as Robert Cooper, the CBC Ombudsman, did when he deliberately lodged eleven complaints of withheld information at a meeting of a parliamentary committee in 1975. He cited information refused to citizens about inspection of sub-standard food in a Whitehorse restaurant, about pollution control restrictions affecting a family home, and about operations of the Unemployment Commission. In these and other cases the inquirers were told either that answering them "would not be in the public interest," or they faced lengthy delays obviously meant to stall them.

Another person recounts asking a simple question about when and where a parliamentary committee was to meet (they're supposed to be open to the public). He couldn't get that information from the obvious place to call, the Committees and Private Legislation Branch of the House of Commons. The chief of the branch, Robert Virr, later told a reporter that he had ordered his staff not to answer that sort of question. "If we allowed it, everybody would be calling," he said.

If people want general facts, they can get them by the bushel from Statistics Canada, which turns out new bulletins daily and, for example, distributed 2,750,000 copies of publications between January and November last year, not counting their census material. StatCan has a User Advisory Service which tries to help people ask for the right stuff. Yet it is surprising how often the particular hard facts you'd like are not facts that have been the subject of statistical research.

Information Canada told me just before it died that it was

in the process of developing a fast, fast retrieval system which would let its local bookstores and inquiry centres pull a card and get any document you wanted from any department in jig time. That is, provided the document was "released" for public information. When D. F. Wall of the Privy Council Office recently did a study on "The Provision of Government Information" he expressed considerable hope in the ability of InfoCan to reform itself and become a "central mechanism of availability," and – here we go again – "a much-needed 'mechanism of two-way response' in the regions."

There were always people hoping for much more from Info-Can. The Standing Committee of the Senate on National Finance did a special study resulting in a report in April 1974. It recommended – once more – that InfoCan improve the information services of the departments – while leaving them intact, of course – scrutinize their budgets, and keep up the good work of the Citizen Inquiry Service.

But the studies and reports may be tucked away now with Bernard Ostry's Task Force Report of 1969, the one he called, "To Know and Be Known."

The InfoCan that was.

The aspect of government information now arousing most ire in Ottawa is that so much is repressed and kept secret. There are various categories of confidentiality and the most questionable has to do with information that is simply accumulated along the line as the government works out its policies and programs. The stuff that enters into planning. When people get curious about what their government is planning for them, and try to find out, then they cut too close to the bone, and information is refused. Policy in process is taboo. The government wants to hold it all in until the finished product is announced. Then you can't do much about it, obviously. Your only recourse is to vote against the governing party at the next election, when that particular policy may be drowned among a hundred other factors influencing your vote.

The issue of confidentiality is a hot one, particularly irritating to MPs, particularly worrisome to political scientists, and it makes right-minded journalists get very preachy, even though many of them actually prefer the fun of filching "leaked" documents which can be made to sound immensely more important than they really are.

In guarding their policy processes against prying eyes, the government often gives a topsy-turvy, Alice-in-Wonderland performance. What used to be a "hard fact," printed elsewhere in some news-stand publication, may become "confidential" when it is written into a civil servant's report. Andrew Brewin NDP MP for Greenwood, had an interesting experience of this kind. He lives next door in summer to a research economist employed by the government. When the British government under Harold Wilson was negotiating a "social contract" with trade unionists in a desperate attempt to control inflation, Brewin discovered his neighbour had written a summary of the situation, and asked to see it. "It was mostly taken from the *Economist* and the *Guardian* and things like that," Brewin said. "It was not critical of our government in any way. In fact it hardly mentioned Canada." But the civil servant was called up on the carpet and informed he was guilty of a breach of the Official Secrets Act. Later, his deputy minister absolved him of his guilt.

Mr. Brewin related the incident before the Parliamentary Committee on Regulations and Statutory Instruments one June day in 1975, when "confidentiality" was getting a going-over by Committee Members. Their star witness that day was Gordon Robertson. Brewin said: "[This incident] seems to me to indicate this attitude which is fairly prevalent that documents that are totally innocuous in nature – and informative in nature – should not be disclosed."

Whereupon Robertson said: "Technically this probably was a breach of the Official Secrets Act."

Mr. Brewin: I must tell you that in my view as a lawyer, I would totally and flatly disagree with that.

Mr. Robertson: I see. Well, as I say, I have not seen it.

Mr. Brewin: I think that would be an extraordinary application of the Official Secrets Act.

The most astonishing things are kept secret. All the particular facts about CIDA, our $750-million aid program to developing countries. Information about CIDA programs is refused, either to Members of Parliament or the public.

Ice damage to fishing gear on the Atlantic coast. Jack Marshall, Conservative MP from Newfoundland, asked for a copy of a report, and was refused.

A letter from former Justice Minister Otto Lang to Secretary of State Hugh Faulkner opposing a grant to a Saskatoon counselling service which gave women information on getting legal abortions. Gordon Fairweather, Conservative MP for Fundy-Royal, asked for a copy of that letter, and was refused.

A research paper into salaries, prepared by Statistics Canada, which the Canadian Union of Public Employees wanted to use as reference. They couldn't have it, though the same paper had been passed out to another group.

A study on single-parent families prepared by the Department of Health and Welfare was refused to a research worker in the voluntary organization, the Canadian Council on Social Development.

A report of the Interdepartmental Committee on Heroin Control was refused because it later formed the basis of a Cabinet document.

A great many of these documents are leaked to the media or to Opposition MPs. There are so many leaks that a special section of Mr. Wall's report was devoted to the subject. Mr. Wall commented that leak-happy public servants are not usually tracked down, and if they are, there is no legal basis for the oath of secrecy they have taken and hence no way of chastising them!

Yet documents are still solemnly labelled Restricted, Confidential, Secret and Top Secret. Who has the authority to label them, precisely how they are to be kept confidential, are very woolly questions. If you want to know just how ludicrous all this can get, you'll find it in a later chapter. The court case in which Walter Rudnicki sued the government was a landmark in the vital issue of government secrecy.

Regulations greatly affecting the lives and movements of ordinary people are also frequently kept secret. Andrew Brewin handles a lot of complaints from people having trouble with

Immigration. He says he has asked for and been refused the manuals giving explicit rules followed by immigration officers. A Canadian may think he has the right to bring in his fiancée from another country – only to be told that according to the secret manual a fiancée means someone he has made arrangements to marry *within six months*. A landed immigrant may have established "domicile" in Canada and may go off to study elsewhere, only to be told when he tried to come back that the secret manual cancels "domicile" after one year. An Occupational Demand Guide is much used by Immigration to decide how many points to give prospective immigrants, based on employment requirements in Canada. But immigrants, and MPs, are not allowed to see that Guide.

In the Gatineau Park area across the river from Ottawa, a large section of land was expropriated to make a zoo. Residents were upset by expropriation and asked to see the feasibility study that led to selecting their area. Their request was refused.

People as diverse as Ralph Nader and Gordon Fairweather have railed against our federal government's obsession with secrecy. Nader, as guest speaker at a Canadian Purchasing Conference in 1975, said bluntly, "Canadians suffer from what I call the Official Secrets Act syndrome. Until these secrecy acts are repealed Canadian consumers will continue to suffer."

Gordon Fairweather, the Conservatives' civil rights stalwart, wrote in the *Globe and Mail* in 1972, in a hard-hitting reply to a speech by Gordon Robertson, that there are some obvious kinds of information that need to be kept secret, bearing on security, or involving claims by or against the government and still in process, or affecting the privacy of the individual.

But beyond that lies "a vast quantity of information which should be subjected to scrutiny and comment – some of it is nonsense, more of it is tentative and will easily be recognized as such, and the availability of most of it would help the public judge the efficacy of policy decisions," Mr. Fairweather wrote.

And he hit the nail on the head when he added, "The tendency in recent decades has been for the executive to interpret the public interest more in terms of its own efficiency than in terms of popular control."

Professor Paul Thomas of the University of Manitoba who served his time as a parliamentary intern in his student days wrote persuasively,

> . . . public argument about the details of a policy at an expert level is an aid rather than a hindrance to efficient government. Plainly, the greater the amount of secrecy, the greater the temptation to rest decisions on a limited number of premises or objectives . . .
>
> It is my thesis that the executive should not define unilaterally what Parliament shall see and hear, yet the Order Paper is loaded with notice for production of papers which are regularly denied by the government on the basis of confidentiality . . . Data is locked away in the Secret and Confidential vaults in the East Block.
>
> I seek, *what I thought was promised by the present government,* a contribution by the public directly and indirectly through its representatives of ideas and opinions about policy . . . Bureaucracies, no matter how technically competent, are not always a good source of fresh ideas.

How thoroughly this approach is discounted by our government is revealed in the evidence of Gordon Robertson before the Standing Joint Committee on Regulations and Statutory Instruments that June day in 1975.

Robertson said: "I find it very hard to see why one should consider that advice or opinions by officials or ministers should and must be public."

He said, suppressing a shudder,

> Government is very, very difficult. If one tries to impose on government . . . the need to do everything in the open and the need to have all advice, all information, all discussion available to scrutiny, I think effective government is going to become much, much more difficult.

Donald Rowat had told the Committee about the Swedish system of laying out the Prime Minister's correspondence for the press every morning. "I regard [that] as appalling," said Mr. Robertson.

He said he thought the Ministers were entitled to their privacy like anyone else – as though public affairs were the "private" concerns of these gentlemen.

He was stoutly backed up by a Privy Council official, Dr. Gordon Smith, who testified, "It seems to me that it would be very damaging if we had a process which exposed the inner workings of policy-making to the public view."

Damaging to whom?

That Standing Committee of Parliament had been assigned the job of going into a subject close to the heart of veteran Conservative Gerald Baldwin, who had been bringing in private bills session after session on "the right of the public to information concerning the public business." Baldwin wants all documents made available as a matter of principle except for a very few relating to national security or individual privacy, and he wants the right of appeal to the courts if the material isn't provided. The government pointed out that since 1973 there have been "Guidelines" – sixteen of them – protecting various types of information; everything else is now supposed to be available. Unfortunately the guidelines cover just about anything you want them to.

The Wall Report was released for the first time to the Committee on Regulations and Statutory Instruments in June 1975. The Privy Council officer, D. F. Wall, had been asked to study the matter late in 1973, and had produced a sprightly report in April 1974, more than a year before it was released. Even then, it appeared minus certain passages which had "been excised," according to Robertson.

Wall pointed out that Canada's classification of confidential documents began in wartime as protection against espionage and doesn't make much sense today. He frankly conceded that too much is inaccessible. He tried to modify the sixteen categories for secrecy into eight new ones, but ended up with very broad groupings. Mr. Robertson said the Privy Council had been struggling with Mr. Wall's report but so far hadn't figured out how to make his criteria work.

Gerald Baldwin posed a question to Gordon Robertson. He read "a statement from a very high authority in the United States":

'A first ground is a valid need for protection of communication between high government officials and those who assist them in the performance of their manifold duties. The importance of this confidentiality is too plain to require further discussion. Human experience teaches that those who expect public dissemination of their remarks may well temper candor with a concern for appearances and for their own interest to the detriment of the decision-making process.'

Baldwin said he thought that was pretty close to Robertson's position, but it happened to be the claim put forward by Richard Nixon for refusing to turn over the Watergate tapes. Would Robertson have advised a Prime Minister to refuse to release tapes of that kind?

Robertson said, "You ask me a very nasty question, Mr. Baldwin."

The United States amended its law in 1974 to make such documents more accessible to the public. Down there they call them "sunshine laws," and California, for example, has had a sunshine law for about ten years prohibiting secret meetings of any public body of any size or consequence. Some U.S. politicians are trying to get back their pre-Watergate privacy, claiming as Robertson does that disclosure interferes with efficiency. But there's healthy resistance – most people feel the officials are being unduly nervous and will find there's no real impairment to efficiency in "letting the sunshine in."

Sweden has had an open system for many years: the constitution says:

To further the free interchange of opinion and general enlightenment, every Swedish citizen shall have free access to official documents . . . This right shall be subject only to such restrictions as are required out of consideration for the security of the realm and its relations with foreign powers, or in connection with official activities for inspection, control or other supervision, or for the prevention and prosecution of crime, or to protect the legitimate economic interests of the State, communities and individuals, or out of consideration for the maintenance of privacy, security of the person, decency and morality.

In Sweden every finished departmental report is made public, whether or not the government acts on it. Of course critics say that a controversial report may be a long time getting *finished,* and it is also possible that a great deal of discussion takes place over telephones. But there's no doubt that much more government stuff gets out to the public in Sweden than it does here.

Canada originally modelled its rules on Great Britain's, but has refused to pay much attention to recent British trends. An important judicial decision in England in 1975, by the Lord Chief Justice, Lord Widgery, lifted restraints against publishing the Crossman diaries, an intimate look at government operations when Richard Crossman was Minister of Housing. Crossman wanted to lift the curtain because he thought most political memoirs are so bland as to be in fact untruthful.

Since the Canadian provinces were never under the same wartime strain as the federal government, secrecy regulations were not imposed – at least in the western provinces. But Ontario, for one, has secrecy restrictions, despite efforts by NDP critic Donald MacDonald to get them removed. MacDonald's bill would give the Ontario Ombudsman the job of deciding whether a citizen's rights have been violated if he is refused a document he wants at Queen's Park.

Ed Schreyer's government in Manitoba is remarkably informal. No document, even a draft of the provincial budget, is stamped "Confidential." Schreyer shrugs and argues that a stamped document would very likely turn up in the Winnipeg *Free Press* next day.

But the government at Ottawa draws the blinds all the way down. It keeps out prying eyes. It also means that an artificial light prevails in the policy-making chambers of government.

It is one more evidence of the sharp pivotal swing away from those bright days when Trudeau ascended the throne in 1968.

Back in 1964, a year before his first election to parliament, Trudeau was saying, "Democratic progress requires a ready availability of true and complete information. In this way, people can objectively evaluate their government's policies. To act otherwise is to give way to despotic secrecy . . . "

In 1968 he listed as a top priority: Information. Two months after his election as Prime Minister he set up a Task Force on Information.

Seven years later his chief public official is firmly resisting the whole concept of openness and accessibility. Private citizens are regularly refused an opportunity to read reports prepared in the Ottawa labyrinth at their expense on subjects of vital importance to them. Information Canada was dropped after a poor try.

If only there had been some visible move in the promised direction! Instead, those indignant cries of consumers wanting to know why Bell Telephone needs another rate increase, those rejected questions put by MPs on the Order Paper in Parliament, that foolery as newspapermen triumphantly reveal the contents of leaked memos, show us a Prime Minister and his ring of advisers stubbornly denying the public's "right to know."

The Trudeau group has decided it is more important to get things done in their fashion. (What happens is that the process is slowed down by their mechanisms; there has never been a government that moves as slowly as this one.) But the important thing is that to decide the argument in favour of *efficiency* is to put us all at great risk.

We arrive at an exchange in Parliament in April, 1976 when the Opposition asked Trudeau to bring into Parliamentary Committees and present to the public the various economic options he claims are being studied for the post-controls period. The Prime Minister said, "The fact that we do it in secret seems to me to be a prudent way of doing it."

As Douglas Hartle put it: "The conspiracy of silence that prevails in our federal and provincial governments seems to me to put their continued existence in jeopardy."

Yet even if these things were changed: if a Freedom of Information Act cut through the confidentiality – we would still have only begun the route to participatory democracy. One of the dangers is the delusion that to inform is to create involvement. It was Trudeau's illusion when he greeted the first draft of the Task Force report with wild enthusiasm. To break the secrecy barriers and give out accurate information is only preliminary.

Far closer to the heart of it all is to open up the channels back into government decision-making – even if we have to use the ugly jargon of the PMO and call it "feedback."

5 What's a "Good Citizen"?

A good citizen is one who stands on his-or-her own feet and knows how to use his-or-her tongue. Who has some know-how about communicating, organizing, and inter-relating with authority. At which point a good citizen becomes a pain in the ass to a government.

The Citizenship Branch of the Department of the Secretary of State had been slumbering for decades. It was concerned with flags and insignia, pomp and show, and certificates for New Canadians. But after 1968 all that changed. Gérard Pelletier, friend of Pierre Trudeau, was Secretary of State. Jules Léger was Under Secretary of State (Deputy Minister). Bernard Ostry was Assistant Under Secretary of State in charge of the Citizenship Branch. Michael McCabe was his Director of Program Development. There were others.

The budget bounded upward. Funding citizen groups to be better citizen groups was the new game. Largesse was dispensed to stiffen the backbones of the less articulate, the least self-confident: the blacks of Nova Scotia; the Métis of Alberta; runaway teenagers heading for Vancouver; hesitant, too-gentle ladies' groups everywhere. To make them into participating citizens.

The citizenship program, like Information Canada, had its decline and fall. Its biggest item was Opportunities for Youth (OFY), which paid out $35 million in fiscal year 1973-74, at which point it was transferred to the Manpower and Immigration Department. When the program was set up in 1971 there was some discussion in Cabinet about where it belonged. Should it be run by Health and Welfare under John Munro or Manpower and Immigration under Otto Lang? Pelletier, who saw its value as a self-motivating (hence, citizenship) employment scheme, won the philosophical argument and OFY went to his Department.

It developed as a program for otherwise unemployed young people, who thought up projects to serve the people of their communities and paid themselves minimum salaries to carry out the projects. They helped blind people, poor tenants, ex-cons – that kind of "client" – as well as carrying on some less altruistic projects. It was supposed to give the participants a chance to express in social action the ideals of youth. They shared the philosophy of the Company of Young Canadians (CYC), started earlier under Lester B. Pearson.

One of the inevitable results of these projects was a straining demand for more and more money to meet community needs.

In December 1975, when the government was looking for things to stop spending money on, the CYC and the OFY were dropped, along with a travel and exchange program in the Secretary of State Department which promoted cheap cross-country tours for students. About that time Trudeau started talking about the New Society, replacing the Just Society he had promoted in 1968.

Some of the old hands would say the CYC and OFY had outlived their usefulness. One very prominent party Liberal said that the OFY had clearly achieved its purpose because it had co-opted the rebellious youth of the sixties; there weren't any of that kind around anymore. This, in his view, had been the only excuse for inaugurating such a program. OFY tamed radical youth. Now the government could get on with its affairs in good old pre-'68 style. Anyway, the fight had gone out of Canadian young people.

Yet it was not entirely a cynical exercise. It seemed for a while there, after 1969, that the people at the Citizenship Branch really saw virtue in helping the unorganized, or the poorly organized, get a solid base for themselves in the community. They used the threat of violent radicalism to the hilt in extracting funds from the Treasury for their programs. The Black United Front of Nova Scotia got its funds after Secretary of State field officers whispered of visits to Canada by members of the terrifying U.S. Black Panthers. The Kent State massacre was always mentioned in hushed tones of pure horror in advocating aid to Canada's wayward students. The Citizenship Branch people congratulated themselves on this strategy, and saw themselves in league with the disadvantaged.

The Branch took to funding native groups, along with "the ethnics." That raised a storm with the Department of Indian Affairs and Northern Resources. It's true the Citizenship Branch was dealing with "non-status" Indians and Métis, those who were not registered Indians and hence not the concern of Indian Affairs. But their manner of funding was far more liberal; the control was more relaxed, the objective was, of course, to let the native groups develop skills in organizing. This ran counter to the philosophy holding sway over at Indian Affairs, where there was a great sense of accounting to the taxpayer for charity bestowed. Indian Affairs felt threatened. Soon some of their clients – registered Indians – were getting money from the Citizenship Branch too, on various pretexts.

They still do. The Citizenship Branch went in for "core funding" – hundreds of thousands of dollars – to let the native people set up their own organizations which then proceeded to zealously lobby the government. That's how the National Indian Brotherhood, the Native Council of Canada and Inuit Tapirisat began, and how they continue to function. The Indian Affairs Department went ahead with "service" programs to their registered group of Indian people – though things were getting tough because the Indians didn't want to be serviced; they wanted to handle the money themselves for education, band development and various economic projects. Relations between the Native Citizens program over at the Secretary of State Department, and the Indian Affairs Department down the street, remain touchy even today.

The Indians obviously find some advantages in this division of effort on their behalf. Unfortunately for them, the climate is changing now at the Secretary of State Department where the Native Programs' section has been checked in growth, some parts of its budget cut, and grants much more severely scrutinized under the "restraint" program.

The native groups have dug in their heels more successfully than other newly created citizen organizations. But, talking to them today, one is told that they still work in the fear that they are somehow being *had,* or they speak of ground lost when a degree of trust established with one official is nullified by a new appointment.

The story of citizen group funding reached its peak in the first Trudeau term of office, between 1968 and 1972. By the end of those four years, cries of "subversives" living on government handouts were raised most particularly by backbench Liberal MPs from Quebec. During the 1972 election, when it was seen that OFY, CYC and LIP (Local Initiatives Projects) recipients did not loyally fight for the government's return to office, but in fact in some instances seemed to favour Opposition candidates, the fat was in the fire.

Funding of citizen groups was all downhill after 1972.

Pelletier had begun to withdraw from the scene intellectually and emotionally, by 1972. He was in serious self-conflict over Trudeau's handling of the October Crisis in 1970, and he was never as close to Trudeau afterwards. Hugh Faulkner, less philosophically inclined toward building independent and participating citizenship, took over as Secretary of State. Jean Boucher, a more hard-headed man than Léger, became Under Secretary. Ostry moved on.

And in the minds of more junior staff members like Cam Mackie, Michael McCabe and Jennifer McQueen, the work of the Citizenship Branch had come full circle. Now they could see that what their subsidized citizens inevitably turned to, as soon as they developed a little muscle, was a demand on government for more power and a fairer distribution of income benefits in Canada. Where else might they be expected to direct their new-found citizen skills?

Typically, money was given to let them organize conferences where the "client groups," intoxicated by this new freedom, passed gut resolutions about welfare, housing, day care, food prices. The resolutions were typed up and sent to one or more Ministers. End of project.

Now the Citizenship Branch activists saw that it was all very well to set out to *equalize opportunity* for such groups to express themselves – to say, "The bankers and the manufacturers can get to government any time. We'll help these other guys (and women) to make their voices heard."

Back came the organized, asking for new laws, new programs, deep changes. Professor Doug Hartle, at Treasury Board in 1972, warned the Secretary of State people that they were merely raising expectations that couldn't be met, because no massive redistribution of wealth and power was about to take place.

So the game went sour. And some of the staff moved off to other departments, thinking they might find happiness in governmental tasks other than teaching citizens to knock on closed doors. Cam Mackie went to Manpower and Immigration, Jennifer McQueen to Museums, Michael McCabe to Central Mortgage and Housing, then to Consumer and Corporate Affairs.

One person stayed, and fought to stay. There is a section of the Citizenship Branch called Women's Program. The acting director, Suzanne Findlay, had industriously cultivated all the scattered women's organizations, high and low, left and right, the Imperial Order Daughters of the Empire and the National Action Committee, creating for the first time some kind of register of organized women in Canada. The objective of the section as it operates under Ms Findlay is "to encourage the development of the full potential of women as citizens in a society based on equal opportunity for men and women." The mandate is to help women "work for change," to improve their relative position in society. Early in the history of the Program the distinction was made between women's service clubs and women's groups working on policy – with a considerable bias toward the second group.

In late 1974 the position of Director of the Women's Program was filled, after a Public Service Commission competition, and the appointment did not go to the acting director. Suzanne Findlay appealed the appointment, on the grounds that her supervisor, Maurice Héroux, had unfairly intervened in the competition. He was reported to have said she was "too close" to the women she was dealing with: she did not subscribe to the adversary system.

Ms Findlay was supported in her appeal by women's groups who contended that she was head and shoulders above any other applicant. Her appeal was granted. The appointment was cancelled. She was reappointed as "Chairperson" of the Women's Program.

Then came 1975, International Women's Year. The Women's Program split the $5-million IWY budget approved by Cabinet with a special Privy Council Secretariat (which produced the "Why Not?" buttons and advertisements). With her half, Findlay organized a series of seminars called Interchange '75. There were seminars on Women and Politics, Rural Women, Women and the Media, Women and Human Rights, Learning for Transition, Women and Voluntarism. About thirty picked women of high calibre attended each session, and so did "resource people" including on at least one occasion Cabinet Ministers, deputy ministers and presidents of political parties.

What came out of the seminars were resolutions – and exasperation. The resolutions were in most cases very specific. (Example: That the Government of Canada introduce affirmative action legislation requiring the Public Service, Crown Corporations and Agencies, and all enterprises conducting business with the government to the extent of $50,000 in any fiscal year to ensure that their female employees are paid on the basis of "equal pay for work of equal value," and that all government tenders stipulate that successful bidders must include this guarantee prior to contract approval.)

By the time the series had reached the "Women and Voluntarism" seminar the exasperation had reached the level of an exchange of hectic wisecracks, and a wall poster listing points of emphasis emerging from discussion started with: "To tell women's groups that they contribute to 'participatory democracy' is both false and a slap in the face." The women at this seminar protested that the resource people who were there to assist their deliberations were people with no power to act on their demands: they were representatives of an array of intermediaries like the Status of Women Advisory Council and the Law Reform Commission which allegedly gather up citizen complaints and convey them to government. Those who had attended previous seminars offered little comfort: they said there had been nothing gained when the Cabinet Ministers, deputy ministers and party presidents had been in attendance. The "resource people" dropped in, listened, expressed their sincere interest, and departed. Whatever happened at the IWY seminars, it was not to be taken seriously as "input."

Ms Findlay, however, thought she was making progress with "resource people." The first time it had been tried, at a conference in 1973, the civil servants invited in to advise and confer with delegates from outside were terrified and wouldn't open their mouths.

Findlay had been so concerned about this gulf that she had tried to get the functions of the Citizenship Branch broadened to include educating fellow bureaucrats in the ways of communication and consultation – "sensitizing" them to the big outdoors. But Ostry would have none of it; he wasn't prepared to take on a task of such proportions.

Even when organizing her IWY seminars Findlay had met resistance. The lists of participants were checked at the PCO; two names were rejected and dropped from the invitation list.

The women's Program group has been amply funded thusfar. But money isn't the whole story. The staff feels they are very far down the list as attention-grabbers at the centre of government. "Sometimes you either get priority, or you get money," was one comment I heard.

What does Suzanne Findlay do next, with International Women's Year over and forgotten? Well, she herself has gone off temporarily on a French immersion course. No doubt she will return to chart the course anew. But in fact one more section of the Citizenship Branch must face up to the limits of what it seeks to accomplish. Once more a group of citizens has been brought to the point of participation. That's all. Shall we gather at the threshold?

What the Citizenship Branch did not and could not do was

6 Paid to Advise

Since government planning became legitimate – mostly since the Second World War – it has been considered appropriate to set up advisory councils. They come in many shapes and guises. But the basic idea is that the councils be not composed of civil servants, but of people preferably with some expertise in the matters on which they offer advice, and above all stalwart, independent and forthright in their opinions.

As it works out these barnacle groups are ignored most of the time.

For example, the most prestigious of the lot, the Economic Council of Canada, brought out sage advice against wage and price controls in its 1975 Annual Review.

Dr. Arthur Smith, an economist with one of the best reputations in Canada, was head of the Economic Council in the years when it did its best work. In late 1969 he disagreed with the hard line the Finance Department was pressing successfully with Trudeau for that earlier war against inflation which led so quickly to massive unemployment and was reversed a year later. Smith's advice in 1969 was not only rejected; he was treated to caustic disparagement by Trudeau's advisers and by Trudeau himself. To a reporter in June 1970 Trudeau said: "I suppose he (Smith) is repeating *his line* . . . "

There is also a Science Council, which achieves a similar degree of success in persuading the Canadian government to nurture home-grown scientists and researchers instead of letting them drift southward to the United States.

It has been fashionable in Ottawa, especially since Trudeau came on the scene, for various departments to appoint small advisory councils with citizen representation. The council members are not full-time; they get their expenses paid and a per diem allowance to come to meetings several times a year. The meetings are, in general, a waste of time and money. Their impact, if we must be frank, is zero.

Such councils are a mere hoodwinking device at least 50 per cent of the time. They are announced with fanfare and they are included in a Minister's speeches when he talks about interpreting the needs of the populace.

A new emphasis was given to advisory councils after Trudeau became Prime Minister. The latter-day cynicism of his regime is painfully apparent when you examine what has happened to them since.

The biggest hoax is the National Council of Welfare.

It is supposed to represent the poor. Sighing, we remind ourselves that about one in five Canadians is still officially and statistically poor – without enough income to meet minimum living standards in Canada. The relative position hasn't changed since the Economic Council (under Dr. Arthur Smith) issued the widely read Fifth Annual Review of 1968. The Economic Council doesn't talk about such things these days: it talks about income averages instead. As a society we are much more incensed about the cost of welfare than about the facts of poverty. So we don't want to hear any more hard-luck stories. Go away, go away.

What hope for an Advisory Council of the poor? Leave aside the crazy idea that their advice might have been sought when Trudeau imposed his anti-inflation program (which froze family allowances and held down wages, but left food, housing and fuel exempt from price controls). No, Trudeau did not call together the National Council of Welfare for a serious talk about what the Anti-Inflation Board might do.

What might surprise us more is that neither did Health and Welfare Minister Marc Lalonde summon the National Council of Welfare for a good round-the-table look at the important legislative changes that were drawn up in his department (but foundered in 1976 when the provinces – Ontario in particular – rejected them). The Canada Assistance Plan which is the umbrella for all the joint welfare schemes with the provinces has been up for major review for several years, dating from Lalonde's 1973 "Working Paper on Social Security in Canada." During those years Lalonde under prodding from his Assistant Deputy Minister (A/DM) agreed to meetings with *professional* associations like the independent (in name at least; it subsists on government grants) Canadian Council on Social Development, to consider aspects of the proposed legislative change. But how about its own little in-house *advisory* group, the National Council of Welfare? Lalonde hasn't spoken to them since that fifteen minutes he spent at the reception following their last general meeting.

So, you ask, what is the National Council of Welfare doing?

A first effort to establish a Council was made in 1962 by Conservative Health and Welfare Minister J. W. Monteith. This Council dragged its heels and was seldom heard from, but during Trudeau's first term of office, in 1970, a brand new version emerged. The startling innovation was to include some real live poor people on the Council – though their presence was tempered by an equal representation of professional social workers. The poor would establish their credentials by actually living in subsidized public housing or by receiving incomes from welfare and below the poverty line. All were chosen and appointed by the Department.

It was at least a move to realize the Trudeau promises of a Just Society and Participatory Democracy.

According to the terms of its creation in an amendment to the Department of National Health and Welfare Act, included in a massive Government Reorganization Act in 1969, "It is the function of the National Council of Welfare to advise the Minister in respect of such matters relating to welfare as the Minister may refer to the Council for its consideration or the Council considers appropriate."

The government accepted those last five significant words in an Opposition amendment from Stanley Knowles, NDP MP for Winnipeg North Centre. They meant the Council needn't wait around until the frosty Friday when the Minister would refer something to them to work on. It meant they could initiate *studies,* and this they have done. Research studies, written in the main by "consultants," have been issued, some urging a Guaranteed Annual Income, some talking about poor kids, or nutrition. Some of the studies have drawn public attention, briefly, to the problems.

The National Council of Welfare was kept alive largely through the persistence of curly-headed Len Shifrin who was until recently its liaison with the Department. Its longevity (five years) was noted as a remarkable accomplishment by two young social scientists at McMaster, Brian Wharf and Allan Halladay, who set out to do a report ("The Role of Advisory Councils in Forming Social Policies," released September 1974) on the various citizen advisory councils but found most of them in such a sorry state (infrequent meetings, no records) that the National Council of Welfare looked like a "success" by comparison. The two authors noted with approval thirteen published reports and quoted newspaper editorials responding to them, as an indication that the Council was an effective voice for the poor.

But what they could not prove was that the deliberations of the Council had ever at any time influenced the formation of policy.

Yet this was its only clearly stated purpose. The Act said so, and the 1970 Annual Report of the Department, commenting on the creation of the Council, said so more succinctly. In the Report the bureaucracy confessed that social services had historically failed to involve the people they served, so the newly constituted Council, with heavy representation from those on the receiving end of social measures, would undertake:

> to advise the Minister; to provide a vehicle through which the poor can make their views known to government and provide a forum in which these views can be considered by a body which encompasses all elements in the social service spectrum and on which the poor will have substantial representation.

Nothing in there about research studies. But that's the way the Council went. If Stanley Knowles hadn't got that amendment into the Act, allowing them to initiate their own ideas, they would have died of ennui long ago, because advise the government they do not.

They staged a big Poor People's Conference in Toronto in 1971 but that was the best thing they ever did, in the considered opinion of most members. Wharf and Halladay interviewed some frustrated Council members who said even the subjects chosen for research were wrong; what they should have researched was "the rich and how they got that way."

A seminal decision at a Council meeting in its first year was to forgo access to "confidential" information in the Department in exchange for the right to publish. The decision climaxed a hot debate exacerbated by those activist members who not only did not want to be muzzled but wanted the Council to take to the streets. The trade-off was established, and the Council was removed one degree from any significant inner workings of the Department.

Thereafter, the Council was a public relations group, adding studies on the poor to other studies on the poor issued by other, better-equipped groups. Some of the more radical members kept proposing that they lead local demonstrations and drum up support for things like a Guaranteed Annual Income. The Council as a whole put down such notions.

The Council's point of contact with the Department continues to be only its liaison officer and its occasional meetings with the Minister present. It has made no attempt to get to know or influence the senior (or junior) civil servants who toil and moil on policies and draft legislation out in that government complex of buildings called Tunney's Pasture.

Marjorie Hartling, executive director of the National Anti-Poverty Organization, is a member of the Council and described its operation this way: They always invite the Minister to attend their meetings, and he actually does attend part of those meetings (biennially) when there are new appointments to the Council. When a report is released it goes to the Minister with a letter and he sends a letter back. Sometimes he uses sections from the reports in his speeches.

Wharf and Halladay got a comment from Marc Lalonde about the role of the Council. They wrote: "The Minister said that when it comes to the question of impact on policy, the Council has input, but he would not go so far as to say it had influenced government policy."

With Council members Lalonde was even more cagey. He confessed to them that he really didn't need their advice, since he whole-heartedly agreed with all their needs and aspirations. "What you people have to do," he told them, "is convince all the die-hards and rednecks out there. You are our salesmen."

The sad tale of the National Council of Welfare.

Leonard Shifrin says there was no other way for the Council to go. The resolutions they formulated were global. They affected the Department of Finance and the Department of Justice as well as the Department to which they were linked. They all led toward a massive redistribution of wealth in Canada. Was that so unexpected?

If an advisory council is to be worthy of the name, it should be able to make two modest claims – it is consulted by the government while policy (and particularly legislation) is in the planning, and it has to its credit at least a couple of occasions when the government altered some decision because of its intervention. The National Council of Welfare flunks out.

And with regret I look at the Advisory Council on the Status of Women, and it doesn't measure up either.

Like the National Council of Welfare, it has been fobbed off with a public relations job and spends its time researching things and issuing statements. It reacts to government measures after they are made public, slapping Trudeau's wrist for not going far enough. It has no inside knowledge of what is being hatched in the way of legislative or administrative change affecting women.

So it too is a hoax.

It is not what any layperson understands by an "advisory council." It is not what the Royal Commission on the Status of Women envisaged in 1970 when they urged that such a council be appointed.

The Council on the Status of Women has two full-time well-paid officers and a staff of eight in Ottawa, and it has thirty members, who get a nice per diem expense allowance and travel expenses when they attend three-day meetings four times a year.

Members keep reminding the Minister and the public of many unfulfilled promises, and particularly the recommendations of the 1970 Royal Commission. They even published a booklet called "What's Been Done?", showing that only about one-third of the recommendations, and those the minor, inexpensive ones, had been tackled.

When the Council tries to enumerate the changes in the status of the two sexes over the past three years, it's kind of pathetic that they have to fall back on the "Omnibus Bill" (passed June 1975) which lumped together a lot of small amendments to various Acts. Half of them directly benefited men.

Thus, through the Omnibus Bill, a husband may now claim support from a wife financially able to support him. A husband can claim a Civilian War Pension as the dependent of a disabled pensioned wife. A husband can also claim a dependent's benefit when his wife dies if she has contributed to the Canada Pension Plan. A wife also is now subject to prosecution as an accessory if she aids an escaping criminal husband.

The first fruits of freedom from discrimination.

The Council was blunt, but totally ignored, in urging reconsideration of the Morgentaler case. In January 1976 one of the two male members of the Council, Claude-Armand Sheppard who is Morgentaler's lawyer, resigned from the Council in protest because their intervention on the doctor's behalf has been ignored. The Council at its first meeting reaffirmed the position the Royal Commission had taken on abortion: that it should be removed as an offence under the Criminal Code. The imprisonment of Morgentaler as an admitted abortionist, the refusal to grant him parole at the normal time, and the threat of further prosecutions stirred the Council to protest. The fact that the Quebec Appeal Court had overruled a jury trial acquitting Morgentaler added to the outrage of his supporters and admirers both on and off the Advisory Council. But the government turned a deaf ear.

The Council studied the need for reform in the rape section of the Criminal Code. When the Justice Minister brought reforms to this section in a bill last year, Dr. Katie Cooke, then chairman of the Council, was so disappointed she called the reforms "piddling."

During the long discussions between officials of several departments about a federal Human Rights Commission, the Advisory Council on the Status of Women has been kept outside. They could only react when the bill came into Parliament, and issue their own version of what a Human Rights Commission ought to be.

Meanwhile, they have been asking in vain that the federal Labour Department amend its regulations to give women equal pay with men in federally-controlled industries. The government says the matter will eventually be written into the Human Rights Act, so why bother with any changes now?

These have been among the Advisory Council's main concerns. With the government they've got nowhere.

And periodically we get another dejected press comment from the Council about the latest figures in job levels in the civil service. Despite exhortations, promises, Equal Opportunities programs and liaison offices, the number of appointments of women to senior levels is tiny, moving up by one or two new individuals from year to year.

Dr. Cooke measures success in "keeping women's issues before the public." Is that an "advisory council"?

Once, some years ago, D.C. Corbett wrote an article on "The Pressure Group and the Public Interest," published in a volume titled *Canadian Public Administration*. He listed a number of reasons why a government might set up an advisory committee. Some of those reasons were to contain public pressure, delay action, pass the buck, shelve responsibility or disarm political opposition. If you're hunting for a reason why we have a National Council of Welfare and an Advisory Council on the Status of Women you may find it there.

Undoubtedly the motives were mixed, initially, at least in the case of the welfare council. But as it looks in 1976 there is no reason except hokum to keep these two groups afloat.

Business Advice

The Department of Industry, Trade and Commerce maintains a Minister's Advisory Council from the business world. Without close knowledge, I can only rely on reports that the Council has been somewhat more active and effective than others.

It works at an obvious advantage. The pervasive wisdom is that what is good for business is good for the Gross National Product. What is good for people in receipt of social services is, on the other hand, on the debit side of the books. Much as social scientists may argue that "investment in human resources" pays off, the evidence is not conclusive in dollar terms. Given this fundamental bias, it follows as naturally as the river flows that incentives to business may be justified more readily than incentives to alcoholics, paraplegics, women entering the labour market, or Indians wanting their own schools.

If you are looking for an Advisory Council with a good line to the Minister, it's safe to say you'll be more effective in Industry, Trade and Commerce than in Health and Welfare.

Consumers

A consumers' advisory council has as long a history as any of these other creations. It is however attached to a Department (Consumer and Corporate Affairs) where it turns out to be on the low end of the see-saw. The genius who first decided to combine both consumer and corporate interests in one department must be accused of schizophrenia. It's the Lion and Lamb department of government. Inevitably most attention goes to smoothing out the wrinkles in business practice to try to maintain the mythical "free market" – constant work for five years on a still un-passed Competition Bill, for instance.

At a conference of the Public Administration Institute late in 1975 Sylvia Ostry, newly appointed deputy minister, said when you looked at the Consumer side of the department, it was "infinitely more complex" and before you knew it you were into questions of "distribution (of goods) and equality." Again, too close to the guts for easy therapy.

But consumer concerns were among those pressing demands for greater democracy taken up by Trudeau's new regime after

1968. The Liberal Party in 1970 noted in a study paper the rise of consumer protest: "the anger over obsolescence, unscrupulous pricing, unreasonable advertising, bad workmanship, high advertising-low real cost marketing." All of which had led to citizens' groups like Pollution Probe, and a housewives' boycott of beef.

The old Consumers Council was moribund. It was perked up, reorganized, after 1970. It continued to lag. When it met there were terrible hassles. Harold Buchwald was chairman. His family connection in Manitoba is staunchly Conservative, and he entered with zest into the role of government critic, issuing statements to the media with a fine, free hand.

Herb Gray, as Consumer Affairs Minister, 1972-74, fretted and eventually slowed down the Council's activities, and just before a new Minister, André Ouellet came on the scene in 1974 the whole thing was disbanded and a very different council emerged. The Minister's press release (April 11, 1974), by some odd mischance, announced as a quote from the Minister's lips that "Although the meetings of the Council will be confidential, there is no restriction on Council members expressing their views publicly on any matter that they consider of concern to consumers, including departmental programs and policies." According to present Council members, it just ain't so. They have been given to understand, very clearly, that they must keep their mouths shut.

The pre-1974 Council went down fighting: its last official act was to proclaim it *must* retain the right to publish public statements. But what emerged in April 1974 was a split into a small private research group (which has done very little to date) and a new Canadian Consumer Council – without the right to publish.

André Ouellet told me that he "wouldn't like them to come out publicly" with opinions on departmental policy. Ouellet has now left; Mackasey didn't keep the portfolio long enough to give the matter much thought.

The Canadian Consumer Council today consists of twenty-four members, meets four times a year, has a very small budget, and is quite, quite different from the various councils preceding it.

Four times a year the members of the Council receive copious material in the mail, including some papers marked "Confidential." These are draft legislative changes, for example in the Competition Act and the Bankruptcy Act. It meets over a Friday and Saturday when the Minister can be present. André Ouellet, during his regime, came, sat and listened. There were departmental officials there too, at about the A/DM (very senior) level.

The Council meets as a discussion group. It doesn't try to agree on any position, it doesn't resort to anything as decisive as a vote. But the members can and do talk. In return for this intimacy they are obliged to keep quiet about what's said.

For the Minister, says Ronald Lang of the Canadian Labour Congress, the Council is a political sounding board. It gives him a valuable indication of what the Opposition MPs and the pressure groups in the private sector are likely to say when the bill hits the Commons.

But, says Lang, by the time the draft legislation reaches the Council it's almost in its final stage, and too late for much basic discussion of what it ought to contain. The Council's job is to react to what the department has prepared, like a wine-taster before the bottle is offered to banquet guests.

That's the way André Ouellet saw it too. "I take them into my confidence," he said. "Relationships have been excellent. I find it very useful – an excellent sounding board."

It seems to me this Council comes closer to being a real advisory body than any of the others. It consults with the Minister and senior officials at one stage (very late) in policy-making.

Ronald Lang can point to efforts he made to see that wages owed to workmen get priority when a company goes bankrupt, in the drafting of the Bankruptcy Act (still undergoing revision). Marjorie Hartling can add that she upheld the rights of low-income people going into personal bankruptcy under the same bill. Maybe, along with other advocates, they succeeded in getting some points across.

Besides, says Hartling, a very practical woman, you can get your lobbies organized if you have some advance knowledge of a bill that's coming up.

David Kirk, executive secretary of the Canadian Federation of Agriculture, says the Minister probably doesn't learn much that he couldn't hear through his own department, or directly from organizations like his own. Kirk qualifies the value of the face-to-face chats.

Kirk was also a member of the Consumers' Council before it was reorganized, in the spring of 1974. Before that it was stormy and "quite ineffectual," he says, but he still favours the idea that a Council should be able to act on its own judgement and issue public statements.

Why should an advisory council, to gain genuine access to a Minister, be sworn to silence? It's all part of the secrecy mystique that prevails on Parliament Hill.

The Consumer Council may be closer in its role to a genuine advisory group in the government structure. But it is small, without a budget or staff, unbalanced in any real claim of representing people as consumers, and above all hamstrung by the tight restrictions imposed by the Minister.

When David Bond was executive director of the Consumers Council, before 1974, he gave a lot of thought to the "consumers' advocate" idea. Everybody is a consumer but nobody is enough of a consumer of any one product – not enough to get heavily involved in fighting against expensive shoes or for a fair deal at the gas pumps. So somebody should take on the job of representing all consumers.

What the government did was put some money into the most solidly established private group in the field, the Consumer Association of Canada (CAC) for an "advocacy" program. The voluntary organization that most directly represents Canada's poor, the National Anti-Poverty Organization, says the CAC is too middle-class and doesn't pay enough attention to the cost of hamburger. Nevertheless it's the government's chosen instrument in this "advocacy" experiment.

What the advocates do is whip up a case against increases in Bell Canada rates, and present arguments before those hearings of the Canadian Transport Commission (or, now, the Canadian Radio-Television and Telecommunications Commission) (CRTC) when Bell requests rate increases. (Only an example. This has been the single biggest piece of action so far. Of course the CAC didn't convince the Commission. Bell Canada always gets its rate increases approved.)

When the idea of consumer advocacy comes up, we are right into the thick forest of the regulatory agencies which have so much to do with public decisions affecting us all. Railway and air fares, what we see on television, whether we build roads or railways, how much we pay for gas.

Besides all the acts of Parliament that allow very important regulations to be made by the Cabinet, without coming back to Parliament at all, there are scores of very big items that are left to be settled by a Board or Commission, completely outside any political control. There's the Radio-Television and Telecommunications Commission, the National Energy Board, the Transport Commission and something like one hundred others. They were set up to be independent – the thought being that they would somehow be purer if they looked like a court, before which the companies concerned must come to argue their case for licensing, rate increases and so on. Over and over again they've become the captive of the industries they're supposed to regulate, and approval is almost automatic.

That's why the mouse's squeak of consumer advocates is now heard at some Board hearings. They will never be an adversary equal to the big companies they oppose. But two representatives of the Law Reform Commission were recently at pains to point out to the Canadian Transport Commission several ways in which the citizens' groups can squeak a little louder. The CRTC, they noted in a brief, sometimes pays the costs for similar groups to come to its hearings. The CTC might do likewise. It might even work the cost into the rate structure it sets – fair enough, since the cost would be passed on to consumers at large who would ultimately be paying for the group that speaks for consumers at hearings.

Something ought to be done, the same brief said, about "court-like proceedings" – the National Energy Board is particularly overpowering to citizen groups who "in their attempts to present alternative approaches, such as a 'social cost' analysis of exporting electric power produced by thermal generating plants . . . have not experienced the same degree of cooperation from the agency that regulated companies appear to enjoy."

Still, citizen groups ought to try to fund themselves, since this is "the basis of their legitimacy." The brief doesn't favour an established advocacy system. Subsidized interventions, the law reformers say, "will probably lose some of their longer term impact because being subsidized requires conformity to previously established standards which inevitably reflect a static view . . . " Too, too true.

The approach of citizen groups can be made easier by other devices to lessen costs, such as providing documents cheaply, and encouraging lawyers to act as counsel for reduced fees. But the only decisive resolution of the problem will be to change the whole regulatory agency system into something accountable to Parliament and the public and, just as important, to put some different members on the boards.

When John Turner (some of you may remember John Turner) was Minister of Consumer and Corporate Affairs he said, "I've looked at a lot of regulatory agencies, and the longer I'm around here, the more I believe that every one of these tends, in a period of time, to reflect the interests of the industry it is supposed to be regulating."

Michael Trebilcock, chairman of the CAC Advocacy Committee, said there were a lot of things wrong with these semi-independent boards, including their membership: "The tendency to retread retired political warriors and reward party bagmen by appointing them to positions on agencies, and the added tendency to appoint personnel with backgrounds directly or indirectly related to the regulated industries, on the grounds that they alone possess the requisite expertise, discounts the need to find appointees of high intellectual calibre with a wide range of social sensitivities."

But are we getting a little far afield? The earlier (pre-1974) Consumers' Council did seriously consider for itself an advocacy role before regulatory agencies. The government decided to subsidize the private CAC instead. So we have the present-day Canadian Consumer Council – advisory, yes, but in a closely restricted, highly informal and individualized sense. Its chance of developing any extra muscle looks remote indeed.

7 The Queen's Quiz

From time to time Members of Her Majesty's Loyal Opposition in the House of Commons demand that a Royal Commission be established to reveal the facts about something limping or askew.

From time to time the government announces with great magnanimity that it is about to set up a Royal Commission to permit a full and impartial investigation of some new or changing problem.

Again motives are mixed, especially on the government side. The simple purpose is to stimulate and sound out public opinion, and conduct research, preliminary to an important revision of policy. More devious possibilities: a Royal Commission may be a stall, a way of postponing action for a year or two or more. It may be a safety valve to let excited citizens sound off and get their opinions in the papers, harmlessly. Or it may be an attempt to get what looks like a consensus for something the government intended to do all along.

At first Trudeau's government scorned Royal Commissions as ponderous, costly, and unproductive. They went in for zippy Task Forces instead. (Perhaps because Task Forces need report only to Cabinet not to Parliament.) They also tried other means, like issuing a White Paper (a British device) to give notice of intentions and invite public reaction before getting on to legislation.

The first Trudeau White Paper of note had to do with tax reform, and it got the Finance Minister, Edgar Benson, and the Cabinet into no end of trouble. Another big one was the White Paper on Indian policy. There have been others, but it helps to see where Trudeau's government is taking us if we look at those two, and three more recent public inquiries: into the Mackenzie Valley pipeline, into Immigration, and into Corporations. (The last a Royal Commission.)

White Papers usually are referred to Joint Committees of the Senate and House of Commons, which hold meetings for as many people as can or wish to contribute to the debate. The proceedings get considerable press and television coverage, and eventually the Committee makes a report which the Minister tables in Parliament. All of this sounds very good for participatory democracy.

Taxes

In November 1969 Trudeau was really not very shrewd about the behaviour patterns of corporate business. But then economics has never been very big with him. He takes a heroic stand from time to time, to "wrestle inflation to the ground" or otherwise inject some drama into the drab economic scene. Thus in November 1969 he vowed to defeat inflation even if unemployment spread (it did) and the unemployed begged him to ease up (they did, and eventually he did).

At almost the same time his Finance Minister whipped out a White Paper on tax reform, loosely based on the Carter Report, which provoked merry hell among the leaders of industry, and caused vast discomfort to Cabinet Ministers who whispered behind their hands that *they'd* never seen the paper before it was aired.

Kenneth Carter, a sophisticated legal brain from Toronto, had been appointed by Diefenbaker in 1962 to produce a proposal for total tax reform, and he had done so in thorough fashion. Carter said our tax system is glaringly unfair: it is much harder on poor people than on rich ones, and it is outdated: it is still protecting resource industries as though we were just beginning to prospect with daring and at great private risk for minerals and oil.

That document hung around while Liberal governments thought up all sorts of other things to do to keep people's minds off it. But Trudeau decided to come to grips with tax reform. His Finance Minister, Edgar Benson, managed to get through two budgets first, but eventually he brought out his White Paper, in November 1969. And Trudeau promised the country that everyone was now welcome to discuss the reforms before legislation was framed.

The White Paper had watered down the Carter Report, destroying the pure and simple structure of Carter's design with a bit of compromise here and there. But a lot of it was still there. For example, the White Paper kept the idea of taxing capital gains (increased value of holdings due to market rise, as in real estate) but introduced ways of modifying the impact. It also proposed an across-the-board corporation tax of 50 per cent instead of the existing graduated rate structure, and eventual elimination of the three-year tax-free advantage the resource industries enjoy. Richard Bird, University of Toronto economist who had worked on the Carter Commission, blamed the government for backing down in the face of threats from the big mineral extraction companies. (Kenneth Carter had died before the White Paper was released.) But Bird thought the government deserved credit for keeping so many of the "core" ideas of the Report, and he said: "But more important than these quibbles is the concrete evidence the White Paper affords of the sincerity of Finance Minister Edgar Benson's desire to remove at least some of the unnecessary secrecy in which legislation has traditionally been conceived in Canada."

These were the last kind words the government heard on their tax reform project.

After a debate in the Commons during which the Conservatives promised a fight to the death, the White Paper went to the Standing Committee on Trade, Finance and Economic Affairs and there it stayed into the following summer.

In Committee concerned citizens came to give the MPs a hand in deciding what taxes ought to be paid, by whom.

The concerned citizens were all the big companies, especially the mining and oil companies, with a panoply of lawyers and economists (all deductible from next year's taxes).

Bill Wilson, *Montreal Star* writer, said the hearings turned into a "snarling national quarrel, all fangs and claws bared." Pat McGeer, West Coast Liberal, said that at his Vancouver club the members were screaming for Benson's head on a platter.

Besides their own briefs, the resource industries enlisted the testimony of fearful citizens who were afraid the companies really would pull out if taxed too heavily, and leave them jobless. They also got support from some provincial governments who had coaxed the companies in in the first place. And bewildered home owners who thought they were going to have to pay a new tax every year if their homes increased in value also appeared to protest.

Most Canadians, though, were blissfully unaware of the whole performance. That May a Gallup Poll showed 49 per cent of those interviewed had never heard of Ottawa's proposals for a new tax system.

Over half the taxpayers in 1967 had incomes of less than $5000 a year, so some redistribution in their direction might seem overdue. McGeer figured the White Paper proposals to raise personal tax exemptions and increase rates at higher levels, with the other measures proposed, would mean "$700 million a year worth of redistribution." The catch was, he counselled, that the tax disincentives would bring business to a slow crawl and be so "counterproductive" that the poor would lose in the long run. He warned Trudeau that he'd be hearing from West Coast and other rank-and-file Liberals.

In June 1970 the Senate got into the act. They decided to conduct their own inquiry, through their Banking Committee. Their objectivity was questioned by reporters who unkindly produced long lists of the corporation directorships held by the Senators. The Senate Committee heard again the corporation briefs, from Hollinger Mines, Canadian Potash, Syncrude, Bethlehem Copper, the Real Estate Boards and the Construction Association. Simply put, said the companies, the White Paper would take us direct to disaster.

The Canadian Labour Congress and the Canadian Welfare Council argued for the poor. But the final tabulation of those appearing before the Commons Committee was: sixty-eight business companies, seventy-six industrial, commercial and financial associations, twenty educational, cultural and charitable associations, eight individuals and a few unclassifiable others.

That summer of 1970, while the procession of lobbyists assailed both Committees and fed a steady stream of threats and alarms to the financial pages of the press, the Liberal party was conducting a quiet little Study Group on Participation. Its "Working Document" talked about the "basic dilemma" of "correlating an organizational society with . . . political egalitarianism."

Donald Macdonald, House Leader, presented his views:

> On the basis of the experience of the White Paper on Indian Affairs and that of Taxation, I think it is important to ask ourselves a number of questions about the success of the technique. Has the technique been a success? Have the public responded by getting into dialogue on the underlying policy choices that face Canadians at large? Will the technique survive to be used again? If I had to predict an answer to these questions, I suspect it would be in the negative . . . In political terms, it may be too costly to engage in such a technique.

(Since assuming the Finance portfolio in 1975, Macdonald has shown no indication of changing his assessment. You know what you can do with your White Papers around the Finance Department. Still, Macdonald has reiterated a view that the budget-making process ought to be somewhat more relaxed than has been customary.)

The Senate Committee released a report on September 30, 1970, urging that the existing tax system, which had done so much to encourage industrial growth in Canada, continue almost unchanged.

The Commons Committee released its report on October 5. In deference to the mountain of testimony presented, what could it do but urge that the White Paper subdue its radiance with just a hint more grey? Equity was all very well, but one must consider the possibility of "an equal or even greater adverse economic impact on the whole private sector of the economy."

Said Tory Leader Stanfield: "The White Paper masquerade is now over."

All that remained was for Benson to translate the "consensus" into new legislation. While the country waited, Benson was desperately reassuring the businessmen who never let up their persuasive petitions. In a letter dated March 23, 1971, he told D.D. Lockhart, general manager of the Canadian Lumbermen's Association, "I do not believe that the present tax rates in Canada have adversely affected the growth of the economy or seriously interfered with willingness to work and I would not expect the proposed new system to change this situation seriously."

And of course it didn't. In June 1971 a bill to wind up the long affair raised tax exemptions a little, brought in a 50 per cent capital gains tax, reduced the amount carefree businessmen could claim on personal expense accounts and entertainment, but left most things as they were. The MPs argued about it long and loud, and Trudeau used closure to cut off debate and get the bill passed.

One of his former Ministers, Eric Kierans, publicly denounced the bill, and has since, outside Parliament, become the keenest critic in the land on over-generous treatment of resource industries.

And Trudeau ruminated. In Parliament he talked about the public participation which had helped formulate the law. Outside the Commons, in a CTV interview, he opined that

> . . . it's likely we heard more from the vested interests than we did from the little taxpayer who didn't have . . . the high-paid lawyers to speak for him . . . I suppose in participatory democracy there will always be some whose voice is louder than others.

That phrase became the title of the book by David Lewis: *Louder Voices: The Corporate Welfare Bums* that carried him and his New Democratic Party into a brilliant 1972 election campaign from which he emerged with the balance of power in the House of Commons.

Was it an elaborate charade? Did Trudeau mastermind a mockery of "participation," to get around the awkward demand for basic tax reform in the Carter Report? Did he, as others claim, mount the big show so he could get away with a more substantial measure of tax changes (capital gains, higher exemptions) than had in fact been brought down for many a year?

I find Trudeau not capable of such high jinks. He can't seem to sustain much of an interest in any economic question, and he could hardly have thought through all the implications of this one. He could simply have left the Carter Report on the back shelf for the mice. He didn't have to bring down the ire of Canadian businessmen on his head, if all he wanted was an excuse not to reform Canadian tax law, much.

I think he tried a big, dumb experiment to support a half-formulated theory of discussion and consensus, and wound up bemused by the discovery that participation is not even-handed because, as someone once said somewhere, money talks.

White and Red

Consultation with the Indian people in Canada takes on an added dimension. Among the Indians there is not only a sense of the right to be heard in a democracy on government laws and policies that affect their lives. There is also a sense of the right to bargain as a separate people who have entered into various forms of contracts and treaties since the time when the whites set themselves up as owners and governors here. The Indians are part one thing and part the other. Part Canadian citizens and part heirs of a separate race with rights not applying to others.

The government got this dilemma hurled at them like custard pie in the face in 1970, and just when they thought they were tidily disposing of the whole "problem."

A huge two-volume report on the disadvantaged position of Canada's Indians by H.B. Hawthorn, "A Survey of the Contemporary Indians of Canada" was published in 1966 and 1967. Nobody paid it much attention, mainly because nobody has been able to read it. But the study had been commissioned because the Indian population was increasing instead of declining; soon there would be almost as many Indians as when the whites first climbed ashore and began wiping them out with smallpox, whiskey and buckshot. The poverty statistics were disgraceful and, worse, they were getting public attention. Churchmen were concerned. Journalists were exposing real conditions on the reserves. It was quite a blow to our pride when international organizations like Oxfam to which we dribbled our charitable dollars began gathering international funds for our Indians.

Friends of the Indians echoed the Indian complaint that the old Indian Affairs Branch, administering the Indian Act, had altogether too much control over the lives of Indians. Indians had to have permission to spend their money, to make wills, etc, etc, etc. The Indian Act, predating Confederation and last revised in 1951, was the framework for administering "Indian lands," the reserve system, and it also regulated the way Band Councils were set up, who could be a registered Indian and a member of a Band, and the controls the Department maintained over Band funds. Nothing much could be done by an Indian except by grace of the department's "agent." The Act perpetuated a wardship. The administration was notoriously paternalistic. Most department agents were firmly convinced that only they knew what was best for Indians.

So here was another area for reform. There would be negotiation with Indians all across the country, and a new deal, so Trudeau promised as he took office in 1968.

The negotiation period drifted along for several months, and consisted of desultory meetings, attended by Indians, who had no prior information except that the government wanted "to change the Indian Act." Harold Cardinal, president of the Indian Association of Alberta, said officials downplayed the importance of the meetings, describing them as "preliminary." A simplistic little pamphlet called "Choosing a Path" was handed out, but largely ignored at the gatherings of natives and government men. When Indians on one occasion asked for legal assistance in preparing their case, the request was turned down by a departmental official who said it "wasn't a legal matter."

Deputy minister John Macdonald saw nothing but political flak arising from these consultative meetings, which in his view were being misused by the Indians to air grievances, instead of to address themselves to the little question outline, "Choosing a Path." He cut short the meetings.

In January 1969 Jean Chrétien, the new Indian Affairs Minister, spoke to the Cornwall Board of Trade, indicating the line the government had decided on. But there was no immediate legislation. Chrétien was being persuaded to publish the policy as a White Paper.

The Indians held a national meeting in April 1969, declaring their firm refusal to discuss changes in the Act without adequate prior study. Of course the old Act should be replaced with something new. But there were some heavy questions to look at first. How good are the treaties in a court of law? When can the Indians expect compensation for lands severed for various legitimate (White) reasons? And above all else, does the native person have an aboriginal right – a right of prior ownership and use of this land, for in the case of the majority of Indians their forefathers had never signed anything to give up what they possessed at the time of the white invasion. The latter question was opening up quite a can of worms. And maybe after all that was threshed out, there could be genuine negotiation and discussion of a new Indian Act, defining the future relationship of Indians within a non-Indian society.

In June 1969 the government released its White Paper. It was quite obvious to the Indians that it had been in preparation for months and they had been by-passed. Where the Indians in April had declared that negotiations toward change were not even begun, the White Paper in June presented a firm package completely reorganizing the position of Indians in the country and inviting Indians to accept it.

The White Paper prepared under deputy minister Macdonald with a strong assist from Jim Davey at the PMO, sounded very good to white ears and there was favourable comment in the press. It declared a state of equality into which the Indians might now enter. It proposed that "the Indian people's role of dependence be replaced by a role of equal status, opportunity and responsibility, a role they can share with all other Canadians."

The catch was that the Indians already had all the civic

equality they could hope for. They had received the blessings of the vote long since. They could and occasionally did run for Parliament; one Indian had been appointed to the Senate. They could serve in Her Majesty's armed forces – and did so whenever the call to arms sounded. They were declared citizens and British subjects under the Citizenship Act and any discrimination against them in any walk of life was clearly forbidden under the Canadian Bill of Rights.

What was really new in the White Paper was that Indian reserves would be broken up and Indians would individually own their little portions of that land, just like white Canadians, to sell it, pay taxes on it, etc, etc. And the federal government wouldn't be responsible for their health, education and welfare services anymore. Such matters would be shifted to the provinces, again to make them the same as everybody else.

As a result, they would be "just like other Canadians."

A remarkable thing happened to the Indians following that White Paper. It had always been an excuse used by Department of Indian Affairs officials that the native groups were totally unorganized. You couldn't talk to them because they couldn't agree among themselves; they had no national spokesmen. Within a year of the White Paper they had a national organization: the National Indian Brotherhood, and it was based with surprising firmness on provincial Indian associations. It's astonishing what a good groundswell of indignation can achieve, along with a little "core funding" from the Department of the Secretary of State. The National Indian Brotherhood (NIB) brought together peoples as diverse as the Nishgas of British Columbia, the Micmacs of the Maritimes, the Mohawks of central Canada, the Sioux and Cree of the Prairie, and a variety of others, speaking other native tongues. The headquarters staff of the National Indian Brotherhood became a small United Nations of its own.

The non-status Indians and Métis organized almost as swiftly in 1971, and the Eskimo (Inuit) later the same year. But these groups were not directly involved in the White Paper proposals.

What scared the Indians most about the White Paper was that it downplayed the treaties and pooh-poohed the very idea of aboriginal rights. The Indians were just one more little old ethnic group in the Canadian mosaic. The White Paper said the treaties only covered about half the Indians of the country, anyway, implying that they were of little importance: "A plain reading of the words used in the treaties reveals the limited and minimal promises which are included in them."

But the Indians of the west were pinning great hopes on the treaties, hoping to broaden the interpretation of the terms to recognize "the spirit in which they were written." The treaties were vital because they were contracts between two separate peoples, recognizing obligation on the part of the white latecomers. Yet now the Prime Minister was saying airily, "We do not make treaties among ourselves . . . ," that is, among different sectors of the single nation of Canada.

As for aboriginal rights, the White Paper dismissed them this way: "[Aboriginal claims to land] are so general and undefined that it is not realistic to think of them as specific claims . . . "

The Indians saw their economic and social needs as so very vast that they could not imagine the provincial and territorial governments happily shouldering the load. Better to keep on laying responsibility at Ottawa's door – at least they would have only one bureaucracy to deal with instead of twelve. And Indians took a sharp look at the plight of the Métis, who *were* under provincial jurisdiction "on an equal basis with other Canadians." "They're even worse off than we are," the Indians said. So much for the joys of sharing the provincial social service systems.

By the time June, 1970 had rolled around, the Indians had mobilized. A large deputation of chiefs came to Ottawa to reject the White Paper and present a Red one. They insisted on seeing the Prime Minister, and other members of the Cabinet. Trudeau's aides advised him against "appearing to undercut Chrétien," but Trudeau agreed to meet the deputation.

Walter Rudnicki then on staff at the Privy Council Office, admits to some behind-the-scenes assistance in the Indians' preparations. Trudeau had just returned from a trip to New Zealand, where he had reportedly been much impressed by the colourful Maori. The Indian chiefs were persuaded to send home for ceremonial costumes and head-dress. They appeared in the Railway Committee Room in the Centre Block not in sober business suits but in full regalia, almost 300 strong, and they opened proceedings with a Cree song of welcome, accompanied by drums. Then in a point-by-point presentation they rejected Chrétien's paper, and answered with their own.

The Red Paper was titled "Citizens Plus," because that was what Hawthorn had called them in his monumental work. It said things like: "Our treaties are the basis of our rights." And "the land [of the reserves] must never be sold, mortgaged or taxed because, as we say, the true owners of the land are not yet born."

At the conclusion Walter Dieter, NIB president, solemnly handed the Red Paper to Prime Minister Trudeau, while a chief tossed the White Paper back to Chrétien. Trudeau picked up the Red Paper. To the Indians, that was an important sign. And, in fact, Trudeau there and then repudiated the White Paper, assuring the Indians that the government had no official policy in mind and was content to wait and work things out, as the Indians wished.

By 1973 he was saying that of course aboriginal land claims were something that had to be taken into account. The Nishga Indians of British Columbia won a split decision in the Supreme Court of Canada and the philosophy of aboriginal rights became valid.

It hasn't been exactly a stalemate since 1970. The Indians, although they've had to fight every inch of the way, seem to be gaining ground in recognition of their claims, and in getting departmental funds (which are steadily increasing) made over to their local administration.

Many at the National Indian Brotherhood complain that the White Paper is still framed in gold over at the Department, and that surreptitiously there's a policy to delay endlessly aboriginal land claims, while they turn services over to the provinces, and gradually assimilate the natives. The government is now tending to spread out its services to Indians over several departments, like Health and Welfare and Central Mortgage and Housing, and to include native people with other groups in these programs. The Indian people fear that when services are directed to low-income whites and natives, the whites get their share first.

There also seems to be a trend in government thinking to let local bands take over the highly divisive question of who is a member (a "registered Indian") and who is not. The effect would be to decentralize and defuse Indian power.

It was a sharp setback to Indian hopes when Chrétien left the Department and Judd Buchanan took over as Minister. Buchanan seemed completely out of sympathy with Indian aspirations. He couldn't be talked to in legal terms, the NIB complained, since he's not trained in law. (He's an insurance salesman.) It was an appointment that said little for Trudeau's commitment to proceed seriously in Indian relations. Mercifully he has now been replaced by Warren Allmand, but his term of office was a low point in negotiations.

The number of bureaucrats in the Indian Affairs Department who still feel the need to denigrate native people is amazing. Back in July 1973 there was a minor flurry when outspoken A/DM John Ciaccia (whom the Indians found generally approachable) said in public and refused to deny that he had said that he "got the backlash from the idiots in the department who hate Indians."

The people at the National Indian Brotherhood have tried since 1970 to establish a method of negotiating change in the Indian Act, and by December 1975 they felt they had succeeded. The delay was largely due to the difficulty in getting agreement from their provincial colleagues; they insisted on such support before proceeding. The way it looks now, various phases of the Act are to be dealt with separately by a government-NIB committee, with the Indians supplying a couple of their lawyers and the government people coming from the A/DM level. There's a "facilitator," Jean Trudeau, at the PCO. It might take up to three years to get agreement on a complete revision, but as each section is negotiated it is to be presented to Cabinet and in this piecemeal way the NIB is looking for progress.

Maybe it really will work.

The White Paper had an effect opposite to its intended purpose. It mobilized Canadian Indians to resist, and to insist on what seems to them a fairer approach.

As far as the Trudeau government is concerned, Liberals now believe Trudeau was even more inept in this White Paper exercise than in the taxation reform process.

The White Paper on Indian Policy was designed for white consumption, full of fine phrases to get white Canadian backing, and drafted in the full belief that the Indians were too dull-witted, resourceless and disorganized to do anything but accept. The Indians turned the tables.

It's no doubt true that they could not have made their "citizens plus" idea stick, if they had not obviously been "citizens minus" in terms of income, health and opportunity. It was the appalling poverty of the reserves, the undoubted discrimination against Indians in white Canadian society, that gave the government and the media and the white public pause. No one was quite prepared to dash their aspirations to special status, when they seemed to have so little else. Now we can see that their cry of nation-in-nationhood poses no threat, if we are prepared to negotiate fairly. A possible course will be a series of settlements which take aboriginal rights into account, and lead to a general improvement, amicably, in the basic social and economic conditions which at present are so far below those of white Canadians.

So this early use of the White Paper was a decided victory for the "client group," and not at all to the liking of certain bureaucrats who would have preferred to push their changes through Parliament and have done with it.

After 1972

The Tax Reform White Paper and the Indian Policy White Paper were produced in Trudeau's first term of office. The 1972 election was a watershed. Trudeau and his advisers were caught up short by their fall from public favour in that election. They abandoned charming concepts of governing through direct contact with the people. And policy control shifted toward the old party politicians and slightly away from Trudeau's computer team.

The 1972-74 Parliament was unashamedly political in character, aimed only at keeping the Liberals in power. If the balance-of-power group had been rightist, we would have had rightist legislation. Instead, Trudeau pandered to David Lewis in Parliament, and he didn't care who knew it. The New Democratic Party kept up a steady pressure, hopeful that a percentage of what it proposed would be taken up by the government.

One of the things the Opposition wanted was a public inquiry into the effects on the Mackenzie Valley resident population and ecology of a proposed new gas pipeline.

An inquiry seemed worth the price to the Trudeau government. A million dollars to appease the environmentalist crowd and the bleeding hearts. This inquiry was not designed to find out anything or to affect anything.

It is the most cynical of Trudeau's ventures into public inquiry. The decision to build the pipeline had been made, under heavy pressure from international oil companies. It was done as secretly as possible, but several fairly substantial accounts of the events have been published.

In 1968 there was a sensational oil discovery by Americans at Prudhoe Bay in Alaska. The men in Ottawa were afraid Americans might lose interest in *our* frontier oil and gas. They were persuaded by the Canadian Petroleum Association that we had absolutely limitless reserves of oil and gas up there, and they didn't want to be stuck with the stuff.

Cabinet Ministers talked to the U.S., ready with tax concessions, export guarantees, longterm commitments, anything needed. Joe Greene at Energy, Mines and Resources and Jean Chrétien at Indian and Northern Affairs spent a lot of time down south talking to legislators and private investors. Digby Hunt, assistant deputy minister under Chrétien, pushed oil and gas export single-mindedly. In June 1975 he was still sounding the word, at a Banff meeting of the Canadian Institute of Mining and Metallurgy, of vast advantages in royalties that governments will reap once the pipeline is in. Jack Austin, former deputy minister for Energy, Mines and Resources, headed a government Task Force on Northern Oil Development, pushing vigorously for a pipeline.

A consortium was set up, to build the pipeline at a cost of about $10 billion. Canadian Arctic Gas Pipelines is made up of twenty-seven companies, mostly foreign-owned. Eric Kierans wrote a lengthy article denouncing Arctic Gas as "a satellite, a pawn, a tool" of multinational corporations and denouncing the pipeline as a bad financial investment for Canada.

Yet hearings are being held before the National Energy Board to receive the applications of Arctic Gas, and another group called Foothills. Not whether to build a $10 billion pipeline, but who's to build it. Meanwhile economists like Eric Kierans tear their hair, protesting the tie-up of capital, labour and resources in a colossal project that isn't needed – by us.

The United States has been losing patience with all this talk and Arctic Gas' friends in Congress have been pushing a bill to get the pipeline authorized and by-pass the deliberations of Canada's National Energy Board and its American equivalent. A treaty between the two nations to guarantee free passage of oil and gas over each other's territory has long been in the works, and occasionally President Ford made little remarks about speeding it up. Another American company, El Paso, threatens the situation with a proposal for a different Alaskan-pipeline-plus-tanker route.

Trudeau did his best to reassure the Americans back in 1973, saying,

> While this project must, of course, be submitted to the usual regulatory proceedings and cannot go ahead until it has been approved by responsible Canadian authorities, the government believes that it would be in the public interest to facilitate early construction by means which do not require the lowering of environmental standards or the neglect of Indian rights and interests.

What did that mean? The government appointed the Berger Commission in March 1974, to "consider the social, environmental, and economic impact of the construction, operation and subsequent abandonment of the proposed pipeline in the Yukon and Northwest Territories."

The native people of the north had let it be known that they laid claim to the land along the Mackenzie, and they wanted their claims settled in advance of any pipeline construction. Northern opposition has persisted, deep, emotional, determined.

Meanwhile, the 1974 election has restored Trudeau to a majority, and an inflexible, position.

Mitchell Sharp, standing in for Trudeau in Parliament, was asked by NDP Member Tommy Douglas just as Berger's inquiry was starting, whether in fact the government would promise to hold up any firm decision on the pipeline until Berger's report was in. The answer was no. Sharp said the government might have to go right ahead, without waiting for Berger.

So Berger could scarcely have started less auspiciously. Possibly to alter the route a shade to east or west, possibly to extract a little more financial compensation to native groups in the final outcome? This would seem to be the most he could achieve. But the British Columbia Supreme Court Judge has conducted lengthy hearings throughout the north, as well as in some southern cities, with a massive, stoic patience that has not failed to impress observers with the hope that his report, when submitted, must somehow carry weight.

Arctic Gas in its evidence before the Berger Commission said plainly that it knew the construction would cause environmental and social damage, but it assumed there would be economic benefits – jobs, civilization – to offset these.

The natives have unanimously said no. They don't get the jobs anyway, except the poor-paying ones. They get the rough shacks and the booze and the prostitution. While their hunting and fishing is imperilled. After the construction is over, the whites pull out, and what's left?

Berger has listened to this over and over. The Indians don't want the pipeline – or they want it on their terms. They say it's their land and the Canadian government has no business even talking about a pipeline until the question of aboriginal claims is settled.

The environmentalists talk about snow goose nesting grounds and caribou walks.

The deep cleavage between the opponents is exactly what a

public inquiry should be all about. As usual, the dice are loaded: civil servants with expertise were forbidden to testify before Berger. Later the ruling was relaxed and they were permitted to give information as resource people if requested, but could not initiate information. And as usual there was trouble with funding. The main environmentalist group, the Canadian Arctic Resources Committee, had great difficulty getting government funds to prepare its brief. In the later stages Berger had requests for extended funding whittled down.

But Mr. Justice Berger has done much to overcome these disparities by giving ample time and opportunity for evidence from the people involved.

The outrageous fact is that he proceeds in the face of the prior announcement by the government that the pipeline will be built no matter what his report has to say.

The Science Council of Canada in January 1975 said, "the pipeline is not for the benefit of the North, either in objective or design." The Council said the government had made its decision to proceed "despite the fact there is so much secrecy surrounding the project no one is sure there are enough proven reserves of gas in the delta or near the shore to support the pipeline." And, finally, "The native people have never been regarded as equals and never been brought into the decision-making process."

"Keep Canada White"

"White Paper" had proved an embarrassing designation for a policy proposal on Indians. Somebody had sense enough to change to a "Green Paper" when Immigration came up for review.

There is no area of government policy where more is decided by regulation, in secret, and less by Parliament, openly, than immigration.

Several years back Canada dropped a quota system which admitted only specific numbers of immigrants from specific countries, or regions of the world. Getting away from a blatantly racist approach, the government set up a point system which admitted immigrants according to their language skills, training, the job prospects in Canada in their line of work, and some special considerations such as having family members or sponsors here, or being refugees from political persecution at home.

The problem is that a lot of the stuff is secret, and immigrants are not allowed to know, for example, whether it's welders or lab technicians Canada needs most. The excuse the department gives for refusing this information is that a lot of would-be immigrants might lie about it, and pretend to be welders or lab technicians. Why it should be impossible to get proof of their job experience and training is a puzzle, to be sure. It does seem to me that the first thing I would ask, if I planned to move to Tanzania, is whether there are jobs for journalists, and I wouldn't think it very fair not to be told.

This is just one area of secrecy. The immigration officers have little manuals, and nobody but they know what's in them. There's a vast amount of discretion left in the hands of the officials.

Somehow the percentage of white immigrants, especially from Britain and the United States, stayed very, very high in comparison to Black or Asiatic people.

The government is aware that most Canadians want it that way. The larger numbers of people from Italy, Jamaica, Pakistan and elsewhere where the skin and the culture are different, have roused some very ugly feeling among Canadians in Toronto, Vancouver, Halifax, and points in-between.

Then there's our persistently high unemployment rate to take into account.

So it's been in the government's mind to cut back. To cut back overall, but to cut back most, as discreetly as possible, among non-white immigrants.

They also began playing around with some very questionable ideas, like compelling immigrants to live and work in backwoods places instead of in big cities. When you begin dictating where certain classes of people, supposedly all citizens or near-citizens, can live within the country, you're into the regimentation we have always righteously deplored in "less democratic" nations.

It's unreasonable to think the government would expect

other, more kindly views to surface in a public inquiry. They could not fail to know that most of the people who would turn up to express opinions would be against more immigration (because of lack of jobs, shortage of houses, etc.) and especially against non-white immigration (because of their private need to be part of a homogeneous group). So to put a show on the road to hear public views on immigration was to look for a barrage of demands for restriction.

The Green Paper on Immigration didn't say a great deal, or give much indication of prior government thinking on the subject. There was to be a wide open discussion. In March 1975 the Special Joint Committee of the Senate and the House of Commons on Immigration Policy was appointed. It was made up of twenty-three Senators and MPs, and they travelled the country, advertising public meetings in twenty-five different cities and letting it be known they'd also like letters and written briefs. They got back to Ottawa and got their report in shape by November.

Not surprisingly the recommendation of the Committee was for a new "managed system" of immigration, with annual "target figures," and a waiting list of approved applicants. The "targets" would be for reduced immigration. Stoutly, the Committee rejected "the view contained in some submissions that Canada should close its doors to immigrants"; it was able to back this up by showing that our population will drop if we keep out immigrants, because our birth rate is going down and a certain number of Canadians leave each year. We need about 150,000 immigrants a year just to stay even.

And it was in the nature of 150,000 a year that the "target" was proposed. This compares with the approximate 200,000 a year that have entered Canada in recent years.

The Committee thought we should keep up the point system which rates applicants according to their "ability to adapt" but leaves so much discretion to officials. It expressed the very proper belief that selection should be on the basis of "first come, first served." But it did not propose any lessening of the secret discretionary power of officials. It said it should be "left to the operation of the immigration system to ensure that undue preference is not accorded applicants from any one country."

The Committee picked up the government's idea of sending immigrants to the backwoods. It recommended that would-be immigrants could jump the waiting list by signing a contract to go for at least two years to some place outside Toronto, Vancouver, and other large cities. How they're to be kept there without unpleasant coercion is not clear. Canadians are showing a marked tendency to leave the little towns for city life. How sensible is it to try to repopulate North Goose Falls from abroad, when the local residents couldn't hack it?

But the Committee, recommending these kinds of restrictions, appeared to speak from a noble stance of non-discrimination and fair play, because it rejected the truly atrocious stuff it had been getting from the public during its cross-country hearings.

Said the Committee: "Some members of the Committee felt that the method had the disadvantage that it elicited the views of unrepresentative and overly emotional individuals." Newspapers and television had reported the violent shouting matches in Toronto and Hamilton between Maoists and a "Keep Canada White" group called the Western Guard. So the Committee had to be merely guessing when it expressed "the confident belief that the majority of the Canadian people are tolerant and generous and not prepared to condone racial hostility and discrimination."

Here's the breakdown of the views they heard: Of 1,629 general opinions on immigration policy, nearly half (48.6 per cent) wanted all immigration, or all non-white immigration, to cease. Another 22 per cent wanted tight controls on the immigration flow. Six per cent wanted immigration based more restrictively on employment needs. Only 7 per cent wanted a more open immigration policy.

The individual letters to the Committee talked about the dangers of non-white immigration in terms of taking our housing, our jobs, our welfare funds, boosting the crime rate and spreading infectious diseases. All these fears the Committee was at pains to allay, using the statistics available, and again could only say, more from hope than evidence, that "it is the persons who are dissatisfied with current policy who tend to respond: those who are comfortable with it are less likely to register an opinion."

Lincoln Alexander, Progressive Conservative MP for Hamilton West, said at an early hearing in Montreal that he had some fear the proceedings would turn out to be "a sham and a farce," and he suspected the Minister of Immigration already had his draft legislation in the works. The new legislation (at this date, not yet before Parliament) would undoubtedly be more restrictive than current policy. Is it nasty to suggest that the Committee was set up to give publicity to a lot of anti-immigration and racist views that would make the government look very tolerant in introducing only moderate new restrictions?

But it was Andrew Brewin, NDP MP for Greenwood, who brought out the oddest circumstance of all. While this elaborate exercise in participatory democracy was going forward, the government was quietly achieving its objective of reduced immigration by changing the regulations!

By introducing a new idea, that an immigrant must clearly not be replacing a Canadian in any job, and requiring a certificate from the Manpower side of the Department to that effect, the government had successfully slashed the number of immigrants by about 40,000 in one year, and was well on its way to getting the newcomers down to about 140,000 in 1976. So who really needed that Committee of Inquiry, except as cover-up?

Corporation Commission
Trudeau has appointed only one Royal Commission during his eight years in office. His early prejudice against Royal Commissions was that they were great time-wasters and merely gave the appearance of action, without changing anything.

It is therefore fair to ask whether these considerations were in his mind when, in April 1975, under pressure to do something about the imminent takeover of the huge Argus Corporation by the huge Power Corporation, he responded by setting up a Royal Commission into Corporate Concentration.

The NDP in Parliament was asking questions. The business world was tingling with the news – the audacious takeover bid by Paul Desmarais of Power to buy a controlling interest in Argus, with its $185 million assets and its diverse, star-studded family of subsidiary firms: B.C. Forest Products Ltd., Dominion Stores Ltd., Domtar Ltd., Hollinger Mines Ltd., Massey-Ferguson Ltd., Standard Broadcasting Ltd., and General Bakeries Ltd. It was considered an exciting coup. Argus shares rose steeply on the stock exchange. To the NDP it was a catastrophic merging of giant power structures which could bode no good for the man on the street – and where was all that government dedication to prevent price-fixing, ensure competition, and dissolve "combinations in restraint of trade"?

In the end, the Power bid failed, in one of the more sensational dramas of the Canadian business establishment.

But Trudeau had a Commission. He gave it a low budget, and appointed three Commissioners and a staff of about a dozen. The appointments told all we need to know about the Commission.

Trudeau chose Robert Bryce, sixty-five-year-old former deputy minister of finance, a former executive director of the International Monetary Fund, long-time adviser to Prime Ministers, as chairman. Bryce has also held the position of Clerk of the Privy Council, now held by Michael Pitfield.

The next Commissioner is Pierre Nadeau, who is, among other things, a director of the Royal Bank of Canada. The Royal Bank was prepared to lend Power Corporation money (estimated at $150 million) to take over Argus. Nadeau was in the front row at the most recent annual meeting of the Royal Bank in Montreal, close by Chairman W. Earle McLaughlin (who had volunteered an unaccustomed public statement a few months earlier expressing extreme annoyance at Trudeau's offhand aspersions on the free market system.) Nadeau clearly has no intention of suspending his business activities, even for appearance' sake, during his term as Commissioner. At the Montreal hearings, when Desmarais appeared as witness, Nadeau asked him whether interlocking directorships were all that bad. Which should get a prize for most leading question of the year.

The third Commissioner is a high-priced Vancouver corporation lawyer, Robert Dickerson, well-known to Liberal party leaders. He is used to speaking his mind, and letting his biases all hang out. During the first day of the Commission's hearings in Ottawa in November, 1975, he clashed with a witness, Robert Bertrand, head of the government office that administers the Combines Investigation Act. Bertrand said it was difficult to get facts out of corporations, and disclosure should be enforced. Dickerson said that kind of talk made him nervous. He said, "Unless we apply the boot to some bureaucratic backsides, I'll find it very difficult to recommend any more disclosure." He also told the bureaucrat, "Much of the information you now get is worthless anyway. There are so many questionnaires sent out, the businessman who has to fill in another one just scribbles any old nonsense and sends it. He figures you'll never know and it doesn't matter anyway."

Which makes it easier to understand why there have been only four cases brought before the courts under the Combines Investigation Act since 1960.

The counsel for the Commission is Martin Freedman whose early comment was that the proceedings would be in no sense "an inquisition." All they were after was to find out whether the power wielded by huge conglomerates outweighs the advantage they bring to their companies in such things as marketing and management expertise.

The head of research for the Commission is Donald Thompson, consultant for some very big corporations in times past, and at one time an expert witness on behalf of Canadian General Electric, Westinghouse, and Sylvania Electric when these big companies were charged with violations under the Combines Investigation Act. Thompson's most quotable quote as the Commission started was that he hoped business will take the opportunity to tell its side of the story.

This extraordinary array of talent dedicated to furthering very big business in Canada makes up the Commission. Their credentials were publicly reviewed at the first hearing by a pair of left-wing Toronto writers, James Laxer and James Lorimer, who asked them to get Trudeau to round out the Commission by appointing three more people from different walks of life, and adding a second "independent" researcher.

Chairman Bryce in a long reply volunteered the opinion that he probably ought not to conduct any inquiry into "the role of corporations generally or the government generally in regard to energy prices," because he had been so closely associated with energy policy in the 1960s. He thought Mr. Nadeau, because he is president of Petrofina, would feel the same way. With these reservations, Mr. Bryce said, "The composition of the Commission itself is a matter that the government has decided"; they would try to be fair and "we are unable to agree . . . with your proposals for changes in our plans."

In Parliament, Trudeau was questioned by Progressive Conservative MP George Hees about "conflict of interest" in the Commission.

Trudeau had reflected sadly in 1972 on the way corporations used all their money and clout to dominate public hearings with their "louder voices," to the disadvantage of the "little guy." Now, in 1975, he was not even prepared to be wistful about it. The Commission itself would decide whether there were conflicts of interest. It was "inevitable" that people on Commissions should keep up their links with business, and it was even a good thing because this gave them "expertise."

Expertise in what conglomerate mergers do economically and socially to the public interest? For that is the second term of reference of the Commission's mandate. It was set up to:

> inquire into the nature and role of major concentrations of corporate power in Canada; the economic and social implications for the public interest of such concentrations; and whether safeguards exist or may be required to protect the public interest in the presence of such concentrations.

The social consequences part got lost when Robert Bryce interpreted in a press release his view of what they were about to do. They were not going to go into competition policy, foreign investment, the Bank Act, or the Combines Investigation Act, since various other studies were underway on these subjects. That left his area of investigation, as he saw it, to the conglomerates and mergers that take in diversified interests (supermarkets and broadcasting), as opposed to monopolies in one field (all sugar or all steel).

Rushing in to present evidence were the corporation giants with their diverse holdings of food chains, hotels, newspapers, wood products, real estate, financial institutions, and so on. Their testimony is that they have to be big because everything in international business is big; they can help the companies they buy up with capital resources and expertise ("We do them nothing but good."), and there are plenty of government control agencies and no more are needed, thank you.

Who will present another side? There have been witnesses at the Commission hearings who have said that other things should be studied; they have not had the "expertise" or the money for research to make the case themselves. But the points they have raised are interesting. Economist Richard Caves said a conglomerate can wipe out the small competitors of any of its "sub" companies, by keeping its baby afloat while the competitors try to bring down prices. He said a conglomerate can produce a consolidated financial statement so no outsider can tell what's making a profit and what isn't. (How is the Anti-Inflation Board to get around that one?)

Robert Bertrand, A/DM at the Department of Consumer and Corporate Affairs, said boldly that bigger firms have an influence on political decisions. But he didn't want to go into that any further, when Martin Freedman pressed for evidence.

Ken Rubin, a perennial lone witness at such hearings, thought the Commission should find out the effect that monopoly business control is having on the quality of care provided in nursing homes run by private firms.

Speaking to a different forum, an Ottawa conference of the Social Science Research Council of Canada, Eric Kierans said the Commission is incapable of dealing effectively with its subject, which ought to be the "pervasive influence of the big private corporation in society." Kierans said Robert Bryce was "the one person most responsible" for the concessions to big corporations, and recalled a Cabinet committee which diluted a competition bill in one breath and approved tax concessions in the next – both measures to promote the corporate monster now being investigated.

So reporters wrote sourly about the hearings of the Bryce Commission, sparsely attended, politely listening to people like

Ian Sinclair, head of Canadian Pacific Limited, who growled that people should be told that all that stuff about a corporate elite is a pack of nonsense. Lorimer and Laxer had pleaded vainly for financial assistance to non-corporation witnesses, witnesses not able to write off their expenses, as companies do, by way of tax deductions. That way the Commission could get spokesmen for the people living in company-run towns, or Indians suffering lead poisoning from rivers polluted by company waste. Bryce replied that everyone had been invited to appear, and as many as possible would be heard, and expressed mild amusement at the thought that neighbourhood groups, like one he belongs to in central Ottawa, might get it into their heads to appear. He said, "We have decided and confirmed last night after studying your paper that we are not prepared to ask the government for funds to pay expenses of people to submit briefs to us or to pay the costs of their travelling to our hearings."

Bryce also said the research undertaken by the Commission was not going to be "a hunting expedition," to dredge up material that people (like Laxer and his friend) "will be able to find something out of, that will enable them to produce arguments in future." Nor, said he, was he "prepared to play the role of ombudsman" in the corporate world.

Breathe easy, Argus.

It took several experiences with public inquiries and White Papers before Trudeau the Newcomer learned the appropriate role for such things in his kind of government. The White Paper on Tax Reform proved what almost anyone might have expected, that the heavies in the economy would not enter into a Socratic dialogue about taxes with guys earning $5000 a year. And merely by proposing tax reform, Trudeau almost destroyed Liberal credibility with the business community. Businessmen didn't like having to amass their heavy artillery to defend their positions, and they have called him a socialist ever since.

The White Paper on on Indian policy proved something

else, that nineteenth-century liberal preconceptions of equal justice would not be met by hand-clapping and grateful cries from the oppressed. Trudeau's bureaucrats thought they were handing down a noble resolution of the Indian problem – to accept those brown people right into the white Canadian community. They apparently thought there would be palavers with dull-minded, scattered Indian groups, explaining what the White Paper meant, and these simple explanations would be all that was needed by way of democratic consultation. It was quite a shock when the Indians said *No*, just as the mining companies said *No* to the idea of equitable taxation.

So after that Trudeau and his group had less stomach for White Paper kinds of participatory democracy. Obviously you couldn't count on people to come to the right conclusions.

Since then there have been fewer full-dress attempts to take the pulse of the nation. The three more recent ones have been significant. The Berger Commission on the problems a pipeline might create in the Mackenzie Valley continues under the shadow of total impotence, because the government announced in advance that it would quite possibly make its decision to proceed – and it probably had already done so – without any reference to Berger's findings. The Immigration Committee gave public exposure to the racism that exists in Canada, making it easier for the government to change immigration laws in the way it had already decided to change them. The Corporation Commission is the most cynical and the most incomprehensible, for here big corporation representatives are telling a big-corporation Commission things which neither the Commissioners nor the government ever seriously doubted. They are talking into a mirror and nobody else is bothering to look.

8 Lobbying is a Delicate Art

At least six times a year and usually more often, the Railway Committee Room opening from the grand rotunda of the Parliament Buildings' Centre Block is the stage for a get-together involving most of the Cabinet on one side of a table and a citizen group on the other.

A very few, very well-established organizations in Canada have an annual tryst with the Prime Minister and his Cabinet. The Canadian Labour Congress (CLC) has exercised this privilege in a tradition that stems back to the days when the Masters and Servants Act governed labour relations. The CLC refers to it as the Cap-in-Hand session. It is always extremely polite. Even in 1976, when the CLC was muttering about a general strike to protest the wage-and-price control program, President Joe Morris was entirely courteous in presenting his annual brief to Prime Minister Trudeau, who was entirely courteous in receiving it.

Other organizations appearing for the full-dress treatment include the Canadian Chamber of Commerce, the Association of Mayors and Municipalities, and the long-established National Council of Women.

It was president Kay Armstrong's turn for the National Council of Women on November 17, 1975. Her blonde hair was "done," her face solemn, her garb religiously appropriate. She entered the Railway Committee Room in the company of gracefully stylish Pierre Elliott Trudeau, red rose in his lapel, deference to the ladies in his amiable smile. She would have stepped aside to let him precede, he would have none of it and made way for her.

Half the room was filled with TV cameras and lights; the principals responded with just the right degree of propriety, casual but nice.

Then they were lined up, face-to-face. The women of Canada with a supreme opportunity, almost the whole government front bench not ten feet away and all attention. A million dollar occasion, adding up the expensive setting, the media crew and paraphernalia laid on, the hourly rate of pay of the dozen or more Honourable Ministers at their disposal.

Mrs. Armstrong seized the moment to ask if the government would consider controls for hazardous cargo on aircraft.

Why *did* she?

With all the tense problems women face these days, inequalities in employment, overburdening in the responsibility to rear children, discrimination in property rights. In fact, not a block away, a seminar of women called together by the Women's Program section of the Secretary of State Department was agonizing over their inability to get serious consideration by government of the reforms they sought – equal pay, fair abortion laws, day care centres.

The National Council delegation got around to some of these things later. But three of the other things they asked for were already in the law, as the Ministers gently pointed out to them. Afterwards, a Senator took them all to lunch.

The National Council of Women was regrettably inept, an old institution, out of touch but locked in by tradition to the yearly meeting. But other delegations, much more *au courant*, are scarcely more effective in this classical and meaningless "consultation."

Colin Kenny, Director of Operations at the Prime Minister's Office, looks after these occasions. He said they "tend to become set pieces" with "not very good dialogue," but when it was suggested that the organizations did it only for the publicity value he bristled and said quite fiercely that "if they just use the Cabinet as a vehicle for publicity let them get it some other way." Some things are still sacred, and one does not jest about this charade.

What *is* the best way to talk to Trudeau?

Some organizations send postcards, all saying the same thing but signed by different names. Some send heavy cartons of petitions, brought in a van. Some people come by the bus-load and walk around the Hill with rather clever slogans on picket signs. Some announce demonstrations, marches up the broad steps, with a pause there for spirited speeches and song, and some go in for unintelligible antics called "street theatre." These exertions leave the organizations weary but virtuously content that they have done their best.

The Ottawa papers generally have something to say about these appearances, but then Trudeau doesn't read the papers.

The accepted routine for those who are brave enough to attempt a lobby, is to request an audience with the Minister most responsible for your problem, plus the leaders of the Opposition parties, plus as many ordinary MPs as time and person-power will allow. Members of your group are urged to contact their local MPs in a follow-up action, in case any are missed in the first assault on the Hill. The amateur lobbyists almost always enjoy the experience, reporting that the MPs, especially the Conservatives and New Democrats, were extremely interested and grateful to be informed. If you go up afterwards and listen from the public gallery you may be thrilled to hear some Honourable Member transmit his interest into a plea on behalf of your cause, cleverly worked into a routine speech on another subject. If that happens you are furiously indignant because most of the Cabinet was absent and the few MPs in their places were reading or whispering throughout the important passage.

When I ran in a federal election it was flattering to discover that mere candidates are also lobbied. I was approached by numbers of people concerned about the seal hunt in Newfoundland. One night as I left a meeting I brushed against a mysterious figure who slipped me a brown envelope, asking me to "read this later." It turned out to be a copious communication from the anti-gun-control lobby.

So lots of this sort of thing goes on, and some of it registers where it counts, with the secretaries attending the Ministers. If they think it's important, the Minister will be informed. Usually, I'm afraid, both secretary and Minister regard it as one more item cluttering the day.

Books have been written about lobbying. A recent one by A. Paul Ross, *Pressure Group Behaviour in Canadian Politics*, makes an important distinction between successful and unsuccessful lobbies. The successful ones, contrary to what you may have thought, are not loud. They are, moreover. institutionalized, with an office located in Ottawa, and their success results from not making a fuss which would expose their contact in the government and embarrass him.

There's been a rapid growth in Ottawa of offices maintained by large companies for lobbying purposes. On top of that, there are well over a hundred Associations which represent the interests of many businesses or professional groups in a particular field – like the Air Industries Association of Canada, the Apparel Manufacturers Council of Canada and the Graphic Arts Industries Association. Such associations may have a number of functions, but the main one is to keep in touch with government. That's why they're in Ottawa.

And then we get to the professional lobbyists, private dealers in contact and impact. The remarkable thing is that Ottawa buzzes with them, but you can never put your finger on one. No one will admit to being a lobbyist, even though it's not illegal. A straightforward search begins with the Yellow Pages: there is indeed a category called *Consultants, Government Relations*, but it has only one firm listed: Capital Communications Ltd. This firm has been in business since 1972, it does a couple of things like getting out trade publications, and it won't admit to being a lobby either. Nevertheless that's what its president, E.L. Littlejohn, set it up for. He had run an Ottawa lobby for a big chemical company and developed a lot of government contacts; on the strength of these he put out his shingle for other clients (he still represents his former employer.). The work that Capital Communications does was described frankly over the phone as "making contacts with the right people in government for interested clients in industry, and setting up appointments for them. Or if a client is after a government contract, we facilitate meetings." They are *very* busy, despite a number of new competitors in town; one factor is the Anti-Inflation Board, with its interpretative rulings on each case before it, a bonanza for lobbyists.

All Western nations – maybe all nations – have a circle of lobbyists next the seat of government. In some countries, notably the United States, lobbyists are supposed to be registered, and to report annually on their expenditures, to bring their activities into the open. Washington observers say the register is almost worthless: the most effective operators don't register, don't hang around the corridors much, and deal very, very quietly with the people who count.

The people who count, the target of shrewd lobbyists, are not your harmless MPs. The *Financial Post* did one of the few journalistic jobs on Ottawa lobbies in July 1975, and started the article with a quote from a "senior civil servant": "People who really want to guide and influence government policy are wasting their time dealing with Members of Parliament, Senators, and usually even ministers. If you want results – rather than just the satisfaction of talking to the prominent – you deal with us, at various levels." The opinion is verified by the lobbyists (who never refer to themselves that way). The public service is inextricably involved in the subtle arts and dealings of lobbying.

And these are, of course, special interests, pressing for special advantage. The *Financial Post* didn't dodge the essential issue: Is sensible legislation "undercut at times by successful special pleading for very narrow objectives? . . . Does the group that hired the best agent get the best results . . . ?"

The role of the public servant is open to serious question. He, like the lobbyist, is subject to no controls. Clive Baxter, who wrote the *Financial Post* piece, describes one of the rules of the game – the lobbyist always pays when he takes the civil servant out to lunch. Who can be trusting enough to suppose that favours stop there?

But quite apart from bribes, and that's a charge not to be made lightly, there is the readiness of civil servants to listen to these special pleaders. We have finally pinpointed some members of the outside world that certain civil servants enjoy chatting with about their work. The lobbyists who represent really important clients, people of influence and power. Those lobbyists and their clients. The civil servant says he *learns* from these contacts, and I'm sure he does. What he learns is not necessarily in the national interest.

The point is that while such private concerns have always pressed their position on the government, *this* government, under the Prime Minister who promised participatory democracy, has been closing the doors and windows to citizens at large in an increasingly secret operation, but has allowed a whole gang and growing coterie of paid agents ready access to the citadel.

Let's look back to one of the powerful influences at work among federal public servants – Trudeau's expressed interest in recruiting from the private sector to positions at the government executive level. The idea is specifically apparent in the Executive Exchange program. This is a scheme set up to introduce more businessmen to government, with a consequent orientation to business objectives. (Some people from universities are also in Ottawa under the program, but the main group is from industry.)

No similar program, let's make clear, was installed to encourage school or hospital administrators to take government jobs, or farmers or plumbers or poets. The chosen group was the executives from private business. The idea came from the 1968 advisers to Trudeau, those computer specialists who had learned their craft in private industry, and believed government departments would function more efficiently with a little business "know-how."

By 1974 a total of forty-four top level positions were being filled on a two-or-more-year basis by people from industry. They came from insurance companies and banks, Labatt's Breweries, the Quaker Oats Company and Canadian Industries Limited. Some federal civil servants had moved into industry reciprocally, for similar short terms.

The government is proud of this program, apologizing only because it didn't develop rapidly enough. They consider the objective admirable: a closer understanding between top people in the public and private sectors. The result is confirmation of the mistaken idea that "managing" a government department is the same thing as managing a private company. The further result is an excessive affinity between corporate business and government.

Back in 1970 a study group of Liberal party leaders considered the problems of "Participation." While doubts were cast on other popular notions (like White Papers) for the general public, one group of participants was welcomed with enthusiasm, the business community: "The private sector possesses managerial abilities and the public sector possesses the public will and money. Hand in hand they must go forward to achieve the objectives of the nation," said the study group report.

So imbued has this nation been, for generations, with the belief that business knows best, that public servants exhibit an almost instinctive deferential attitude to business pressure. When we examine the imbalance between citizen groups and industries appearing before regulatory agencies (like the Canadian Transport Commission) it's accepted that the government's professional experts may comfortably appear to back up business, but will very seldom "stick their necks out" to testify in support of a claim by a citizen group.

The success of the business lobby was never more clear and bright than when John Turner was Finance Minister.

Globe and Mail. June 7, 1972, Edmonton: In his swan song as president of the Canadian Manufacturers Association, Gerard Filion praised the federal government for coming round to industry's position on a number of economic matters, the free enterprise system for the high level of material benefits it bestows and the CMA for its strength in vigorously pursuing the manufacturers' cause.

At a luncheon at the association's annual convention, Mr. Filion, president of Marine Industries Ltd. of Montreal, was profuse in his praise, of Finance Minister John Turner and the May budget, which was a happy blend of economic realism and social justice.

This is a Minister of Finance who speaks our language . . . He did not deliver more than was necessary, but he did deliver, Filion said.

Business International Executive Services, representing top international businessmen, is a lobby on a grand scale. Put together on one occasion by Elliott Haynes, it successfully persuaded the Pearson government to renege on Walter Gordon's nationalist economic proposals. It was about to gather at another "round table" – completely private, no press, no written record – in Ottawa in April 1972 to talk to Trudeau and his Cabinet about impending foreign investment review legislation (which has turned out to be such very mild stuff that hardly any applications are turned down, and foreign takeovers of Canadian companies continue apace). That particular round table had to be called off in 1972 because the Haynes' memo to the participants, promising them a golden opportunity to influence the Canadian Cabinet, was leaked to the press and got some nasty headlines. We did learn how a really heavy lobby operates. The participating executives were willing to pay $600 apiece for the privilege of meeting with the Ministers in very private small groups "permitting intensely personal interchanges."

Government's relation to business can be seen from many angles. It might seem that almost all government activities relate to promoting "a healthy climate" for business.

Calvin Coolidge said: "The business of the government of the United States is business." Most Liberals, though they demur, respect that philosophy.

So we get preferential corporation tax treatment for new capital outlays; we get transportation subventions or rebates to reduce marketing costs; we get all kinds of public money made available when private credit looks inadequate; we get tariffs; we get trade promotion assistance; and we get a vast expenditure on the roads, bridges, wharfs, railways, power lines and research programs that support business. We even get arguments that family allowances and old age pensions are there not so much to help kids and old ladies as to provide "consumer support" – a large crowd of customers for private business.

In laying on all these helpful programs for business, the impetus of new ideas comes mostly from business lobbies, dealing with public servants.

As an erudite writer in the learned magazine, *Canadian Public Administration*, once put it:

> Most public measures relating to business are not conceived and imposed from the top, but are usually developed in response to specific demands put forward by business and other interested groups. Over large stretches of public policy, government intervenes in business in approximately the same proportion that business intervenes in government.

Businessmen meanwhile complain bitterly that government is hard on them, and never more bitterly than over the anti-inflation program of wage and price controls. It's not so much that their prices are being squeezed, since calculations are based on all their rising costs plus a "reasonable" profit compared to former years. It's a "disincentive" perhaps, but it's also all that infernal paperwork. And it's the precedent of what they regard as unwarranted interference.

The other side of the story, in government relations, is that government must always keep one eye on the voters, few of whom head corporations. While the government subscribes to the theory that prosperous business is the mainstay of the nation, it must also be seen to keep a watchful eye out for everybody. When business thinks government is showing too much concern for other community interest it is very apt to call the governing party a bunch of "socialists" – which in many Liberal hearts produces a warm, virtuous glow.

The business lobbyists of Ottawa were exposed to rare public view with the well-publicized Lockheed affair of 1976. In the deal to purchase from the United States' company, already in bad odour with its own government and the subject of scandal abroad on huge bribery charges, the Canadian defence department was dealing with the clients of a unique pair of lobbyists, Simon Reisman and James Grandy. Reisman was deputy minister of Finance, Grandy deputy minister of Industry, Trade and Commerce, until both retired at age fifty-five (with pensions of about $30,000 a year each) to form their consulting firm. Reisman is chairman and Grandy is president. If there is anything Reisman and Grandy don't know about government, if there are any doors on which they cannot knock or any numbers they hesitate to call, it would be hard to name them. They speedily took on as client the huge industrial corporation of George Weston Limited, and this move was facilitated by the fact that Reisman, a month or so earlier, had been appointed to Weston's board of directors, on which occasion he was introduced to the Weston annual meeting by G. Galen Weston, chairman of the board. Galen Weston said Reisman was the member of the management team who would carry the special function of overseeing government-company relations. For some people, life *begins* at retirement.

The very shaky deal with Lockheed, the difficulties the government got into trying to twist the arm of a group of chartered banks to provide financing, turned the spotlight on the pair of ex-deputy ministers. In Parliament there was talk of a bill to limit lobbying enterprises for a respectable length of time after a public servant's retirement, though the Prime Minister said he didn't think this was "a practical alternative."

What Reisman and Grandy had to say about all this was that they were indeed providing "professional and technical advice" to Lockheed – but they denied that this was *lobbying*. Lobbying, in their view, would be to make the actual requests to government, instead of merely "advising" their clients.

One of the very nicest comments on the intimacy of it all was written by James Grandy in a letter appearing in the Ottawa *Citizen* on April 8, 1976:

> Finally, I turn to the question of the kind of role that can be played by public servants after they leave the government service. Ministers have spoken frequently about the need for better understanding of government by the private sector, and *vice versa*. The government, some years ago, established an active program sponsored by the Public Service Commission to encourage the interchange of executives between business and government. This has played a useful part, but much more is needed. My colleague and I are making every effort to contribute constructively to the objectives of this policy.

Another outstanding performer in this field is Bill Lee. The Reisman-Grandy firm has sometimes been chary about interviews – reporters have been told that business is going well, thank you, and the firm doesn't need publicity, though it certainly got it after the Lockheed affair. But Bill Lee is disarmingly friendly to one and all.

He entered the "consultant" field with his skills well honed. He had been a campaign strategist in two Trudeau elections; and an executive assistant to Paul Hellyer when Hellyer was Minister of Defence. He gets awards as "Man of the Year" for work in the United Appeal Campaign. Now he's president of perhaps the top group of lobbyists in the business – though of course he says they aren't lobbyists – Executive Consultants Limited, with a handsome, handy office in central Ottawa.

Lee dislikes the word "lobbyist" and explains, exactly as Grandy did, that he never presses a client's case with a member of the government; he merely advises the client on the best way to go about it. At the same time he sees a lot of public servants. It's important to keep in touch with the PMO and PCO these days as well. But merely to find out what's going on, what's shaping up, so he can be useful to his thirty or so clients in the business world.

The only point at which Bill Lee really took pause in my conversation with him was when I asked him if any unions were counted among his clients. It took him just a second to find the logical reason for this gap in his portfolio – the unions, of course, deal with government through their own outfit, the Canadian Labour Congress. (Doesn't business have the CMA?)

Bill Lee said that his outfit doesn't do anything so crude as mix with companies looking for government contracts. In a way it would be less equivocal if it did. What he offers his business customers is advice on *influencing government policy*. He knows at what levels policy can be most successfully influenced – somewhere in the middle ranks of the public service executive group. And of course at the PMO and PCO.

Lee says he spends quite a bit of time also telling businessmen how they can be Good Corporate Citizens, so they'll have a stronger claim on government sympathies. He advises them to do things like hiring more Canadian instead of American professionals, using more institutional advertising instead of the old hard sell, that kind of thing. But – Lee is fussy about words – he wouldn't call this *building their image*, it's more a matter of helping them establish a good reputation with government.

When Lee started consulting he had Bill Neville as a partner. Neville had been an executive assistant to Judy La Marsh in Health and Welfare. But Neville was stricken with a strange disease. He decided to run as a Conservative candidate in the 1974 election against John Turner. After that he didn't come back to Executive Consultants Limited. There's no record of any great anxiety to have him back. He had lost his credibility with this government.

The close tie between Liberals and lobbyists was established again in the "consulting" firm run by Jean-Luc Pepin after his electoral defeat in 1972 and before his appointment as head of the Anti-Inflation Board.

There is nothing illegal about lobbyists. They are merely far more successful than most in establishing contact with the Liberal government. Their services are for hire, and business has money to pay them and considers the fee worthwhile. At the same time, the increase in their numbers may indeed be proof that this government is becoming inexplicable even to its dearest friends.

But if we are to see things in perspective, let's drop in on Ruth Bell. A degree in political science. Wife to a former Cabinet Minister. Active in Ottawa political circles. Since 1973, president of the Canadian Federation of University Women, with an Ottawa office "to permit contact with government." Success – zero.

"It takes me eight weeks to get an appointment with a Minister," she said. She doesn't have easy access to senior civil servants, either – that's just as hard or harder.

At the behest of her organiztion, she has tried to get the subject of abortion removed from the Criminal Code. She has tried to have the Indian Act changed to remove discrimination against Indian women who marry white men. She has tried to get the Human Rights bill changed. She has tried to effect

very minor changes, to which there was all-party agreement, in the Citizenship Act. These requests have been
backed by women's groups other than her own. Ruth Bell's
efforts have made no noticeable dint in the solid bulk and
tough hide of the federal government.

The special project of the University Women has been to
get women appointed to government boards and commissions.
There are 143 federal boards, with a total of 1214 people acting on them. Twelve per cent are women. Ruth Bell thinks a
great many more women could be named. Their first overture
met the answer that not enough good women were known to
be available. The CFUW then asked for a grant of $6000 – in
International Women's Year – to draw up a roster. They
worked hard through their local branches and came up with a
list of 360 women, a list complete with biographies and qualifications.

Finding out where the Board positions were and when vacancies would come up was extremely difficult. No one was
passing out that information. No one, it seemed, could say
what the standards of selection are. In the circumstances, the
best Ruth Bell could do was make a stab at seeing the Minister
in charge of known boards, presenting her roster and recommending what seemed the most likely names.

International Women's Year came and went. The grant ran
out. Despite assiduous effort, nobody from their list got an appointment. Refusing to concede, CFUW applied for and got
another grant to continue the roster for a second year. So far –
no luck.

Would the fact that she and her husband are leading Conservatives in Ottawa have any bearing on the matter? Would
being a woman present some kind of obstacle? Ruth Bell is an
above-board type: she says no to both suggestions. It's just un-
believably hard to get anywhere with the government.

Less charitable is Terry Padgham, hot-tempered vivid
young woman from Yellowknife, who says her main problem is
that she wants to press for other than "women's issues." Especially during International Women's Year, one could always
talk to a government person about women's problems. There
was no appreciable result, but one could talk. Try to have

some input on defence issues or taxation, and it's a different story. The shutters bang shut. *This is not for amateurs,* comes through very plain. It's getting worse, Terry Padgham thinks. Between 1972 and 1974 when the Liberals had a minority government, there was much more listening. It's a comment heard often from would-be participating citizens.

"The government wants us to just piss around until we lose all our energy," said Terry Padgham. " 'That's an interesting project. Go write it up,' an official in Edmonton told me. When he got it he said, 'It doesn't fall within our criteria.' They wish we would just go away, have a baby. It's a growing waste of time to talk to them."

Terry Padgham is bitter about the stifling effect of the civil service. She thinks a terrible fate overtakes a battling citizen-at-large who takes a government job. "What happens to to the old *commitment*? There's a lot of co-opting going on. Taking a job puts you in a situation where there's a conspiracy to shut you up." She adds, cryptically, "Maybe the reason we can't get recognition for unpaid work (housework) is because there's so much recognition for paid un-work."

The interesting culmination of a three-day seminar in late 1975 on "Women and Voluntarism" was an urgent decision to form and maintain an Ottawa lobby for women's rights. Called together as one of a series of seminars by the feisty "Women's Program" section of the Secretary of State Department, the delegates represented nation-wide, umbrella organizations like the National Council of Women, the Federation of Business and Professional Women, the National Action Committee, the National Council of Jewish Women. For their networks of local organizations, each of them has attempted over many years to press their views on government. The discussion was accompanied by rhythmic teeth-gnashing.

All present could agree on several issues of major concern – a fair deal for women in employment, removing abortion from the Criminal Code, pensions for housewives. A lobby could speak for many staunch backers with a large number of common concerns.

The public servants who sponsored the conference were disappointed that the urge to lobby did not resolve itself into a decision to adopt *them* in an "advocacy" role. But whatever the zeal of the seminar's sponsors, the women shied away from the doubtful advantages of choosing a champion on the "inside." Somehow, an independent lobby had to be established. Months later they were still facing the problem. How to get something organized without government funding?

The impasse is unresolved.

Marjorie Hartling, on the other hand, has surmounted many of the obstacles in learning to relate to government. She is executive director of the National Anti-Poverty Organization. She started with an office in her own basement in Burnaby, B.C., but moved to Ottawa about three years ago. She has now established some important contacts – she was for example asked to attend meetings of the Committee on Egg Marketing at Herb Gray's suggestion, though André Ouellet's assistant would have stopped her. She finds she functions best in getting pointed questions into the hands of Opposition MPs for use in Question Period in the House of Commons. "The big gulf is between us and the civil service," she says. "It's extremely important to get to them. You don't get far, though, if they don't like you or your ideas."

For low-income groups in search of access, Marjorie Hartling prepared a lobby manual called "Man Versus the System" with as much direction as she could put together. It starts: "Even getting the correct telephone number to make an inquiry is an exercise in frustration."

The women over at the National Indian Brotherhood can also tell you a lot about lobbying. There is Marie Marule, until recently executive assistant to president George Manuel. A Blackfoot from Alberta, a brooding, sober, careful-spoken person, shrewdness and altruism splendidly mixed. For five years she entered into endless conversations and negotiations between the NIB and the government. The Indians have a special approach – "to protect our lands and our rights" – a nation within a nation.

Marie Marule was with the NIB through several major setbacks. One was the appointment of Judd Buchanan as Indian Affairs Minister. Marule says Buchanan frankly believed Indians are lazy and pampered. And an A/DM in the department, P.B. Lesaux (now replaced), also gave the NIB nothing but a bad time, operating always on the adversary system, from preconceived positions. Why these appointments? A relationship that looks promising is destroyed when the wrong civil servant suddenly moves into a vital spot in the bureaucracy. When Jean Chrétien was Minister, the NIB believed it was approaching a *modus operandi*. Because the group knew Chrétien had to take policies to Cabinet, they would go after additional support to back up their proposals to him – they would canvass the Liberal caucus, talk to the press, to the churches. Sometimes it helped. Chrétien has been moved to the Treasury Board, then to Industry, Trade and Commerce.

Marule discovered the basic weakness of their negotiating position was in dealing only with the Department. If an official wasn't listening they were stonewalled. Now they have a direct line to the PMO, "for balance."

Early in 1976 a new consulting mechanism was established with a number of participating Ministers, along with Lloyd Barber, Land Claims Commissioner, and the presidents of the provincial associations of Indians, plus the NIB executive. They deal with a wide range of policy – one priority is the long-delayed revision of the Indian Act, with all its attendant problems of Indian status in the Canadian community.

But how sincere are the government negotiators, Marule wonders. Even while they worked on a policy of socio-economic development for the reserves, a $180,000 contract was being signed with a Toronto public relations firm, Coupples Communication Consultants, Marule said, "to get Indians into real estate dealings, involving land surrender, and joint enterprises with non-Indians . . . So are they doing their own thing while they pacify us by *negotiating*?"

Negotiating brought more results when Trudeau ran a minority government. Marule shares this opinion with many spokesmen for citizen groups.

One government official she respected highly was Norbet Préfontaine, formerly at the PCO. She credits him with staving off a completely arbitrary "final solution" to the Indian question – when the deputy minister of Indian Affairs would have wiped out the Indian Act and forced assimilation through legislation, Préfontaine urged Indian consultation. And as a result he "got scuttled," Marule said. "He made powerful enemies. Why didn't he become Assistant Deputy Minister at Indian Affairs? Or Undersecretary of State? Instead, he's been shunted to International Policy at Health and Welfare."

Her suspicion is strong that this government, through entrenched senior officials at the Indian Affairs department, is still committed to carrying out the intent of the White Paper.

Marule talks of the James Bay settlement, which for the sake of new hydro-electric power to export to New York State, paid off the Indian population in a settlement "not even equitable to last century prairie settlement."

When the James Bay negotiations were going on with Quebec Hydro and the Quebec government, the Indians and Inuit had to defend their case alone. Where were the federal government people who manage to mix into every other facet of Indian existence? "They refused to get involved," Marie Marule said wearily.

The Indian people, though they may feel the constant need to remain defensive, are a tough group of negotiators. They have lobbied, to survive. They fought back from the brink of a policy that would have led to their extinction as a separate people. Now their major battles are for land rights, economic development of their reserves, and for better Indian education under the local control of Indian school boards.

If the "adversary" approach is endemic to all civil service negotiations with the "outside," it reaches its pitch in dealings with the Indian people. Throughout the Department the air of confrontation is inescapable. The department does not want to work *with* the Indian people. It's a fight every inch of the way.

So far, though, a battle of words, with only an occasional sit-in or demonstration by local or regional leaders.

9 The Rudnicki Case

As might be expected, few adherents to "participatory democracy" have survived unreconstructed on the Ottawa scene. Several embittered activists resigned in anguish, usually to pursue careers among their "client groups."

One was fired, in a spectacular display of bureaucratic wrath.

Unlike most people in such situations, he fought back. He challenged his dismissal in court, claiming that he had faithfully executed a promise to "consult" made by his Minister.

The case of Walter Rudnicki is classic in its dimensions, illustrating precisely what I have been describing to this point. Because he upheld the principle of formulating policy in concert with the people to be affected by it, he challenged not only his former employer, Central Mortgage and Housing Corporation (CMHC), but this government's whole way of doing business.

So I've chosen to relate the story of that case as it happened.

I had seldom seen the interior of a courtroom before July 5, 1976, when Walter Rudnicki's case was heard before the Supreme Court of Ontario. For nine days I was to follow it from hour to hour with ascending excitement. I would wonder why people on the street were talking about the Olympics. As a politician I saw in the case a full bag of ammunition to bring down the Trudeau administration in the next election, an eventuality I thought would be very good for us all. As a democrat, I saw the case as a watershed in relations between government and the governed.

Water Rudnicki is a lean, Ukrainian-background Canadian, sharp eyes, grey hair, small moustache. For eighteen years he was employed in the federal public service, rising by stages to a senior level, causing some commotion along the way but never making the news with any public indiscretion.

He has been a friend of my husband's for some years. They share an avid interest in old books and other rare and wonderful objects of historical – if not, in my eyes, always aesthetic – quality. We sometimes see Walter and his wife Simone at their place or ours; my husband had assured me I would like the five Rudnicki offspring and the fact that one or more of them was always part of adult parties. (I did.)

Rudnicki had been fired. October, 1973.

Rudnicki had declared it was a mistake. When he saw it wasn't, he took court action against the government corporation, for wrongful dismissal.

On July 5, 1976, he was seated in the centre of this courtroom, which to me looked much like a chapel to some particularly severe deity, with very hard pews, and no decoration but the Arms of Her Majesty high on the front wall.

Rudnicki, sitting stiffly alone, looked grey that first day, with taut cheek lines. It could be he was obstinately gambling all he possessed (he had had my husband in to help appraise his library a week earlier) at the age of fifty, with four of his children still to get through university, in a futile attempt to save his pride and – what else?

Rudnicki comes from the North End of Winnipeg, an End with a very big reputation as a producer of movers and shakers.

His father and mother came from the Ukraine, met and married in Manitoba, went broke trying to run a dairy farm, lived on the wages of unskilled labour or on relief in Winnipeg during depression years. He didn't speak English when he started school in Winnipeg; he put up a hand when the kid next him did. At thirteen he was leader of the gang on his street – the Aberdeens.

"We never got in trouble with the police, but the gang a few blocks over, the Redwood bunch, were always in dutch. One of our missions in life was to protect the Aberdeen little kids from the Redwood gang."

He told me about one encounter. A challenge laid down by the Redwoods, the Aberdeens taking it up; under a street light the Redwood guys waiting. Rudnicki came, but his gang chickened. The Redwoods dared him, he walked out to meet them. "Where's your gang?" "Oh my guys are around." Visions of many Aberdeens in ambush. A resolution in talk, negotiating territory. Tribal peace.

"Everybody's Ombudsman," Simone teases him. He went into social work, getting his degree after the war.

Rudnicki's speech is clipped and rapid. Not a rabble rouser. A behind-the-scenes performer.

In 1956 he came to Ottawa as a welfare officer to work in the Arctic for the Department of Northern Affairs and National Resources. He discovered that *he,* with two assistants, was the Welfare Unit, created by Ben Severtz, the kindly overburdened head of the Arctic section of the department. So Rudnicki went north to see why Severtz thought the Eskimos needed welfare services.

Tuberculosis patients were picked up and shipped south with scarcely a word to their families. Children disappeared down south. "So I got a system of taped messages and radio communication and yearly visits set up. Keeping families in touch with TB patients. It cost a hell of a lot of money."

Worse things. A very high rate of death or re-admissions when TB patients were returned north. Discovery that they were flown back in down-south clothes. Spending without authorization $60,000 for eiderdown sleeping bags, as regular issue to released patients returning to northern life.

Rudnicki enjoyed, no question about that, the shaking up. And met, head-on, the deputy minister of the department, Gordon Robertson.

Robertson is not the sort of man to cast in a villain's role. He has an Oxonian air, he is steeped in the aura of parliamentary government, British style, with its inviolable concepts of loyalty, discretion and propriety. He is the best close adviser a Prime Minister could dream of, as Pearson discovered later when Robertson served in the Privy Council Office as Clerk. The regular morning meetings with Robertson were invaluable to Pearson, as he generously admits in his *Memoirs,* and Robertson became a diplomatic trouble-shooter when matters needed a fine hand.

There are those who say that Robertson abhorred the Conservative party under John Diefenbaker, and was among those top mandarins who, convinced of Diefenbaker's incompetence, were less than enthusiastic about service under his regime. But with the Liberals back in office under Pearson and then Trudeau, Robertson played an influential role.

His place in Canadian political history may be as the last defender of government in secret. He speaks strongly and with feeling on the subject, and it was for this cause that he recommended firing Rudnicki from CMHC in 1973.

When Rudnicki moved into the Privy Council Office in 1966 Robertson was there before him. In between for Rudnicki – after leaving the Arctic Division – was a stormy period of employment in the Indian Affairs Branch, where he gained his reputation and won his enemies.

Indian Affairs was run in semi-military style within the old Citizenship and Immigration Department, under Colonel H. M. Jones who could, with a finger on a buzzer, cause any junior official to leap to his feet in mid-sentence and scurry to the Colonel's office. But a good-hearted man, Guy Favreau, was temporarily Minister, and Claude Isbister was deputy minister, and with Colonel Jones on the point of retirement Rudnicki moved in to head the Welfare Division for Indians. It was 1963. There was a stir, a new-generation revolution, in North American life. Rudnicki brought it to Indian Affairs, a ripe target.

"Community development" was the new thing, a self-motivating approach to social services, tried out by missionary types in underdeveloped countries with gratifying results. Rudnicki travelled to Peru, Mexico and Puerto Rico on a World Health Organization (WHO) fellowship. He proposed to introduce the same concept on Indian reserves.

He brought in Farrel Toombs of the University of Toronto, under whose direction ninety new people were trained in the art of community development. Their training included a sensitizing three-month period, isolated in a monastery, of self-analysis and re-evaluation. The product, a new civil servant, dedicated to a job and a client, not to the department paying his salary. Innocently as dynamite sticks in folded umbrellas they arrived on Indian reserves, where the only white authority and contact had been the "agent" or superintendent. The pyrotechnics could be seen afar.

The department changed and became Indian Affairs and Northern Development. The deputy minister changed; the Minister changed. Arthur Laing was not Guy Favreau.

Rudnicki moved on.

For three years he was on staff in the holy of holies, the Privy Council Office. He joined as deputy director to a Special Planning Secretariat which struggled, under Tom Kent and Bob Phillips, to echo the War on Poverty making headlines in the United States. It came to a stumbling halt in April 1968. After that, policy adviser to Robert Andras.

Andras received an appointment as Housing Minister and the Minister through whom the Central Mortgage and Housing Corporation would report to Parliament.

Paul Hellyer had resigned from the Cabinet; his Housing Task Force had failed to get quick implementation and he was cold-shouldered. What was wanted was a docile Minister who would leave housing to the CMHC. But Andras had ground to recover. He wanted a portfolio. He decided to develop an urban policy group that could be translated into a Ministry. In effect, to aim for a lot of what was in Hellyer's report: the overview, the federal presence in urban growth. But all he had was the staid CMHC, more of a banking institution than an imaginative city builder. What he needed was pressure on the entrenched officials of the Corporation. In Rudnicki he had the kind of man he needed for that job.

Central Mortgage and Housing Corporation, established in 1946, handled the low-priced Veterans' Housing built by C. D. Howe, but now downplayed such direct involvement: it existed chiefly to guarantee home mortgages through private lenders with additional funding to stabilize and expand the mortgage market. It speeded up direct funding in the late fifties in a deliberate effort to stimulate the economy; afterwards the injection of house-building money to keep industry humming was seen as its real reason to exist.

It also promoted good housing design as a frill exercise, and it had acknowledged a responsibility for poorly-housed citizens with an Urban Renewal Program. That Program brought more bulldozing than new homes and came to an abrupt halt shortly after Andras took office. It was without a replacement.

CMHC was quite a comfortable place to work, semi-independent from government and the civil service, placid. It fiercely resented Hellyer's abrupt attempt to transform federal policy, without so much as a nod or a scrap of advice from CMHC. It was not likely to relish innovations from Andras. Herb Hignett was President, but his term was nearly up. Among those who turned up, expressing some interest in the naming of a successor was a young Ottawa housing developer named William Teron.

But Hignett was asked to continue a bit longer. And Rudnicki, along with activities to get Andras' Urban Ministry established, was at Andras' request doing something he called "building a policy planning capability" into CMHC. Andras put him into CMHC as an executive director. He conducted Task Forces, which probed such matters as sewage, land ownership, and low-income housing. Some of the reports sharply criticized CMHC and were labelled secret and locked away. One author, Michael Dennis, rebelled and published his own report on low-income housing. Another, by Peter Spurr on the role of land speculators in keeping housing prices high, was only revealed in 1976 when it also was published privately.

From the Task Forces Rudnicki was moving to a research and policy development unit of some eighty souls.

They were Rudnicki's *gang*. The potentials for conflict were very real.

Walter Rudnicki had reached a senior level in government, he had acquired a large home on the Driveway, he was passionately interested in the fine pieces of old furniture, rugs and prints it contained, he was party to a desperate but successful bid (with Gene Rheaume) to save the Riel Diaries from going to a United States museum when Canada's Archives refused to pay the required price. His family was thriving.

Yet it was not all that serene. Rudnicki was told that the Privy Council Office kept a Black List, called by those on the cozy inside "The Extra-Parliamentary Opposition." He heard that his name appeared on it as unsuitable for any top position in Canada's public service.

Though he might have expected a step up to the rank of either a vice-president at CMHC, or an Assistant Under-Secretary of State (assistant deputy minister) in Andras' budding ministry, neither came his way; he continued as an executive director in charge of the division he had created.

Rudnicki was not, of course, the only challenger to the established ways of the bureaucracy. Something unheard of was happening in those years – an epidemic of "leaks" of government-stamped confidential material. At first each "leak" was a headline; in a year or two it was everyday stuff. People in the government were slipping the goods to reporters or Opposition MPs. And I think we should take a look at how Gordon Robertson, Clerk of the Privy Council and Secretary to the Cabinet, felt about this, for he was the lad with his finger in the hole in the dike.

Robertson made a speech to the Royal Society of Canada in St. John's, Newfoundland, on June 6, 1972, on "Official Responsibility, Private Conscience and Public Information." He was much disturbed about "leaks"; he blamed them on the new permissiveness and disrespect for authority in society at large. He said the leaks were reported and commented on in "a rather festive mood," without considering their grave importance to public morality and the very basis of our governmental system.

It was his view that no civil servant should put his private conscience ahead of his sworn oath of secrecy. If he wanted to blab, he should resign. As simple as that.

When he described why government papers are confidential he began with the obvious: international relations and defence, and the private business of individuals who have been asked to supply information for census and other records.

But the vast area of policy-making was the main concern. And Robertson contended, and still contends, that every scrap of paper assembled to affect or introduce policy changes, on its way up the line to the Cabinet, must be kept from the eyes of the public.

He related this to our tradition of Cabinet Solidarity. Instead of one executive department we have many, under different Ministers. But the Ministers must arrive at one joint decision, in Cabinet, and then they must all stand behind it, and nobody is ever to know who argued which way, or what the arguments were.

So if there was any public disclosure of any "input" to one Minister's proposal, then the whole thing, he said, would collapse. "To disclose the document would be to disclose a personal view and thus pierce the veil of privacy on which collective responsibility depends."

A suitable period of secrecy for all government documents, he thought, was thirty years.

Speaking of the new values which put a "cause" ahead of one's official duty, Robertson said:

> There is no consensus about what exactly is meant by 'participatory democracy,' and satisfactory techniques which will fully satisfy the individual yearning to become involved have yet to be devised – if indeed they can be.

In his eyes, obviously a matter of far less consequence than to preserve the right of the government to keep its papers secret. His plea was for the group of harried Ministers who, as he saw them, were far from being despotic and overbearing; the problem for them was "not whether to crush or dominate, it is how to cope at all."

Of course there were those who argued with his assumptions. But it would be from real conviction that Robertson would advise the president of the CMHC to fire Rudnicki for permitting the showing of a paper stamped "Confidential" to a group of native leaders.

Rudnicki at CMHC was working among other things on the amendments to the National Housing Act that would augment housing for low-income people – assistance to Neighbourhood Improvement and Rehabilitation to old houses. Following *his* set of principles, he was calling meetings with the people on the receiving end.

Sue Findlay (now with Secretary of State) was at a seminar where a citizen group from Montreal turned up, and CMHC officials were set back on their heels by the forthright demands of these "clients."

And so it was with native housing. There was provision in the National Housing Act to fund groups who wanted to do special surveys on housing needs, and this was used to the hilt. Between 1970 and 1973 a total of ninety-two grants totalling $2,225,000 were made to Indian and Métis groups to set up their own organizations to learn about housing legislation and assess their own needs.

The Métis and non-status Indians are the step-children of Canadian society. While the department of Indian and Northern Affairs had housing programs for the "real" Indians and Eskimos, the Métis got no special treatment. Yet they were desperately ill-housed, slum-dwellers everywhere, on the fringes of towns, out in the bush, or in rundown city centres.

Chetwynd, B.C., about 1969.

A resourceful mayor, Frank Oberle, with an idea that would lead in a direct line to that courtroom in Ottawa in July 1976.

Oberle and his wife Joan, a social worker, elated at their chance to help build a small new community, made a decision. They would not shut out the group of non-status Indians living across the creek in ramshackle homes – "I never saw anything that bad in Germany after the war," Oberle told me – the ghettos that other towns tried to ignore, running their best streets in a direction where the view was easier on the eyes. The thirty-six native families would be part of Chetwynd.

It must be a personal kind of self-help. Oberle knew the Indians wanted a bridge over the creek; he invited them to a meeting to talk about the bridge. Then he talked about other things, about laying out a sub-division with a lot for each family, the town to put in sewer and water. He would give them some gas for power saws, lend them a bulldozer from his farm. To his town council, Oberle pointed out that their municipal grant would go up by $38 a head.

The natives responded. Most of them were on welfare. Oberle set out to get federal public housing money, which was designed for large rental projects. Gene Rheaume from Rudnicki's CMHC group, doing a Task Force report on native housing, was in Victoria. Oberle phoned him, flew down, worked out with Rudnicki start-up money and a special provision as an experimental project, to use the public housing section of the Act for ownership instead of rental units.

The houses, with some skilled assistance, began to go up; at Oberle's insistence each family had to help with the planning and do most of the work, earning $3.50 an hour as "carpenter's helpers," $2.00 going toward the cost of the house.

Halfway through the project, the Chetwynd council rebelled. They took advantage of Oberle's absence on a business trip to get a petition signed and delivered to Victoria, disallowing the sub-division. Joan Oberle phoned, Frank flew back. He "dressed down" the council, threatened to resign. They gave way.

The natives built forty houses. Oberle saw the improvement in the health of native children whose hospital stays were dramatically cut. He saw the psychological lift. He saw the gradual acceptance by the town's whites, and it was a great day when a native man joined the Jaycees.

In Vancouver, a week-long seminar starting June 17, 1973, the culmination of many joint meetings, Métis housing groups now organized in many parts of the country, now in orbit with CMHC personnel. A hard look at shocking housing facts. A resolution to work jointly – the Chetwynd plan – with natives putting in work in lieu of money where they had no income – in on the planning, in on the operation, in on the control.

I talked to John Gasson, then executive director of the Canadian Association in Support of Native Peoples – some time after that seminar. He said he was so exhilarated by the exchange that went on he could hardly credit it. "I'd dreamed for years of seeing it done that way," he said. When told of Rudnicki's dismissal he said, "It's unbelievable."

In Parliament Frank Oberle, now a Progressive Conservative MP for Prince George-Peace River, would ask questions about Rudnicki's dismissal, about the loose definition of "confidential" documents.

Meanwhile, since 1971 Rudnicki had been facilitating a "Winter Warmth" program to bring especially bad native housing up to a minimum standard, to make do for a few more years.

A change of Ministers. In a Cabinet shuffle in January 1972, Robert Andras and Ron Basford switched portfolios, both believing they were being demoted. Andras was told he was to organize the west politically in advance of the next election, so he'd need a lighter portfolio. He agreed under protest: he wanted to carry Urban Affairs considerably farther than he had succeeded in doing to that date.

Ron Basford was equally reluctant to take it on. He saw the move as punishment for the row he had stirred up with businessmen over his Competition bill in his first portfolio, Consumer and Corporate Affairs. The Ministry of Urban Affairs was certainly undesirable: a position with no financial (patronage) clout, a "policy overview" ministry, its relations with other departments and other levels of government still sleazily defined. Basford was in Trudeau's bad graces because he had let British Columbia Liberal interests go downhill; he had even neglected his own riding. It may be true that he was given the Ministry as punishment, until he "shaped up."

(Though I tried both before and after Rudnicki's case came to court, Basford refused to be interviewed.)

Central Mortgage and Housing, the Corporation that reported through Basford to Parliament, was a strong agency with money to spend and a vast capacity for building political friendships. But relations between the self-contained Corporation and the fledgling Ministry were weak, if not hostile. Basford had a rough assignment.

Basford's first brush with the developing native housing policy was in September 1972, when what had been prepared to that date was forwarded to him for possible election use. The election was safely past; no word on the policy came down the pipeline.

Basford stayed aloof from the Corporation: he appeared to be marking time.

And CMHC during Basford's reign was not a happy place. President Herb Hignett was also marking time, near the end of his term. The "old guard" was cultivating Basford and disparaging Rudnicki and his "pinko" group.

At the same time some members of Rudnicki's gang had begun to wish Rudnicki would take the chip off his shoulder; they had been parachuted into the Corporation by Andras, they had established themselves, maybe they should make peace?

The long-delayed amendments to the National Housing Act went through strenuous re-drafting before their passage into legislation in 1973. Their swing to social need instead of sound financial support to the construction industry, meant a dip in the CMHC budget. The Treasury Board, and John Turner in Finance, made rough noises about costly social services. Having just presented slum city areas and dilapidated urban homes with funding help, Basford was unlikely to get a program for native housing through Cabinet without argument.

In July 1973 the appointment of Hignett's successor was announced. This time William Teron was not put off – even though Basford would have made a different choice. Small wonder Basford was nettled. Teron, he knew, would never play the role of *subordinate*. Basford's speech-writers found his temper so volatile at that period that a dozen drafts failed to please.

The appointment of Teron as president of CMHC was made after an "executive search" by a Toronto firm, Canada Consulting. Jim Coutts, formerly a secretary to Pearson, now Principal Secretary to Trudeau, was a partner in this firm. Nobody was flabbergasted when it came up with Teron's name.

Jim Coutts now lives in a Teron-built luxury apartment hotel, the Inn of the Provinces, close to Parliament Hill.

Though he had been on the boards of universities and hospitals Teron had never been a civil servant. He came fresh from the role of private developer. He became an intimate of Pierre Trudeau, became part of a very small group meeting frequently at Trudeau's home, entertained Margaret on a holiday at Key Biscayne, Florida. He played squash with Michael Pitfield, now Clerk of the Privy Council and another close friend of Trudeau's.

"How come he gets on with Trudeau?" I asked a man who knew them both. "He can't be intellectually stimulating."

"Far from it," the man chortled. "Teron is, if anything, anti-intellectual."

A staff member from CMHC agreed. "When Teron draws up his own stuff about housing policy for Canada it's straight Reader's Digest."

Dark, below medium height, well-tailored with just a dash of *mod*; chubby brown cheeks, a way of ducking his head and pouting as he ponders unpleasant matters. Bill Teron grew up in Manitoba, the son of poor parents, and he quit school early. He has the typical self-made man's nostalgia for the humble beginnings he worked so feverishly to escape. His public speeches are dotted with references to his boyhood home and the homey comfort of the rough attic bedroom he shared with his brother. He made his business reputation in Ottawa with an "ideal" community on the city's western outskirts. Kanata has winding streets and kept some of the trees and natural rocks – it was expensive but a lot prettier than the sub-divisions put down by Teron's rival in those days, Robert Campeau. But we get a glimpse of Teron's mind in his personal supervision of Kanata – every resident *must* join the homeowners' association, every resident *must* get his mail at a community post office. Togetherness was the prescription.

"A socially conscious businessman," Basford called him. (Publicly.)

To be housing czar for Canada, after his personal fortune was secure, was an attractive next step for Teron. Who wields more power in the economy than he who decides how many housing "starts" will be made each year? Who but the president of CMHC can finance huge land assembly sites for suburban mini-cities (a thousand Kanatas), all to be built by private developers?

Teron had moved from building expensive residential suburbs to building expensive downtown hotels. On appointment to CMHC he followed the usual "blind trust" procedure by removing visible connections between himself and these real estate holdings, which have nevertheless prospered to a fare-thee-well since July 1973. The real estate group from which he is temporarily divorced by reason of his "blind trust" is Urbanetics Ltd., a very familiar name on construction signs in the heart of the capital; its head office is in the penthouse suite of the Carleton Towers Hotel that Teron built.

Teron reportedly sold his large share holdings in an investment company, now renamed Commerce Capital Financial Corporation, where his associates had been such well-heeled and politically powerful people as Maurice Strong, Jack Austin and Paul Martin, Jr.

Teron bought C.D. Howe's old home in Rockcliffe Village. He was forty-two.

"He's our first *political* president," said a CMHC employee. "Not like old Herb Hignett who always told us to keep our heads down during an election. Teron lets everyone know he has a direct line to Trudeau."

Two things were obvious: Teron had worked too hard and too carefully to be easily deflected from his new "public service" job, and Teron would introduce *his* ideas, *his* pattern of organization, while anyone in determined pursuit of other goals would get short shrift.

And it was September, 1973.

Tony Belcourt, energetic and agile president of the Native Council of Canada, wanted to see the joint-enterprise housing policy so nobly conceived at the B.C. seminar translated into action. He sent a brief to Urban Affairs Minister Ron Basford and asked for a full-dress interview between government and natives. The request was granted. The meeting would be on September 12.

Now we can rely on court testimony, for the September 12 meeting was the first in the events leading up to Rudnicki's "wrongful dismissal." In addition, I took notes from Rudnicki and other participants and I looked at copies of a number of Rudnicki's private papers, which most of the press haven't seen. The trial roused considerable interest.

Several witnesses would tell how on September 12 Rudnicki's Policy Planning people from CMHC, with President Teron, went first to Basford's office to give him a quick briefing. The "Winter Warmth" program was of concern to the natives: could it be expanded? Yes, and the name changed, Basford decided, to Emergency Repair. How about the long-term housing policy? Basford fretted that he still hadn't received one (forgetting the pre-election offering), and here were the natives on his doorstep. He said he wanted a policy by September 21.

On to the large Railway Committee Room where such formal meetings were frequently staged, and there waiting was a full complement of native leaders, from almost every province and the territories along with national Native Council of Canada officers. Basford, Belcourt and Teron at the head table.

A new $2-million allocation for Emergency Repair was promised by Basford. But this was a "band-aid" – literally to patch houses too dilapidated for living, yet being lived in.

The brief from Belcourt. Basford promised a new long-term policy by the 21st.

Protests at once from J. Angus Spence, president of the Manitoba Métis Federation and Stan Daniels from Alberta, interjecting. *That* sounded too familiar, too much like the kind of program they had seen in the past, they said, handed down from on high, bearing no resemblance to their expressed views. This time they wanted genuine consultation.

Assurances from Basford. Did he say "every step of the way" as some witnesses remembered? A hand-written note from Robert Marjoribanks, on Rudnicki's staff, days after the event: "In going over my notes of the meeting with Mr. Basford on September 12, I see that, after telling the NCC that he would have policy proposals from CMHC by September 21, he added: 'However, I might not like some of these proposals and may have to consult with you further.' Exact quote."

Followed by assurances from Teron. The one phrase most witnesses recalled: Teron saying, "This time you won't read about it in the papers." The Marjoribanks' note says: "Mr. Teron said in reply: 'Our policy will take into account what the provinces (provincial Métis organizations) say they want. We will consult with you on any policy. It won't be just an announcement in the paper for you to read!'"

Then they agreed a consulting committee of natives should be set up in Ottawa, and Teron indicated Rudnicki as the man who would work on the policy from the government side.

And some of Rudnicki's men left the Hill that day in a high mood of elation. *For the first time*, genuine consultation. Genuine involvement of the natives – the one vital factor that would make the program work.

Most witnesses were to agree in court on what happened next day, September 13. A meeting in a CMHC conference room with many of the same participants. Even-tempered discussion of the $2-million fund for emergency repair, dividing it among the provinces, but wanting it increased. Then the natives meeting apart from the others to pick their consultation committee. When Teron arrived, near the meeting's end, he listened to the request for additional emergency funds and said he would take them up with the Minister. He heard of the consultation arrangement and approved.

So far, on course.

What happened after September 13 would lead to directly conflicting testimony in court. Successively more formalized policy papers, a half dozen of them. Meetings back and forth, several with the Management Executive of the CMHC to review the developing policy; two with the native representatives to consult.

On September 19 (20?) a quick consultation with Native Council officers and a look at the rough policy-in-progress, which Belcourt pronounced "garbage." What he didn't like was lumping natives and poor whites together, instead of a distinct "native housing policy"; bringing provincial governments into the operation; and excluding those Métis who had moved to town from what was now dubbed a *"rural* housing policy." So Rudnicki took his objections, concisely listed in an Appendix to the draft policy, on September 21 to the Management Executive (Teron in the chair.) No hue and cry about consultation so far.

But Teron would say in court he had no idea the natives were seeing the draft documents as they took shape: "There was no suggestion that this document or any other document was receiving a distribution different from the normal prescribed distribution." How then did he think the natives had been "consulted"?

The natives' objections were not met by CMHC Management, though they agreed natives would get priority treatment under the plan. Urban natives would have to wait. Some minor concessions were made.

A more detailed discussion at another Management meeting, September 25. Still another October 1. They were past the deadline, with successive re-writes. A quick meeting with Teron to straighten out minor points. Now it was close to a finish, and Rudnicki called a "final consultation" meeting for October 5 with the Native Council group. He had other things to discuss with them as well, including a sharp letter from Angus Spence protesting that the consultation process wasn't going far enough.

But on October 3 came the call from Basford for the overdue policy. Hot from the typewriter, the latest draft was handed to Teron, who saw something he didn't like on a page dealing with finances, tore out the page and threw it on the floor, dressed down the drafter, young Lorenz Schmidt, for trying to "manipulate" him, and sent him packing to fix up the draft and bring it to Basford's office. Which Schmidt, much incensed, but consoled by Rudnicki, did.

Teron, though he handed the draft to the Minister with a flourish, hadn't really studied it. So when Basford "joked" about adding his signature then and there, Teron "joked" that it wasn't ready for signature; it was merely for Basford's information.

Once a draft, however unfinished, was in Basford's hands, did it take on sanctity?

Yes, said Teron.

No, said Rudnicki. It was not yet by any official standard a "Cabinet Document."

Thus the issue was joined. The secrecy of government papers was challenged. The preservation, if Gordon Robertson is to be believed, of the very foundation of our good democratic system.

The sincerity of this government in dealing with native people or any group of citizens was also at stake, if Belcourt is right, if Rudnicki is right.

For when October 5 came, Rudnicki let that October 3rd

draft (minus several appendices) remain on a table where the native consulting group gathered for a final session with the CMHC policy people.

Rudnicki says he made some exclamation of surprise when he saw the document, but decided it would be best not to make a scene.

The document on the table, like several drafts before it, bore the labels: "Confidential"; "Memo to Cabinet"; "Property of the Government of Canada."

But what do such labels mean? It is a form used, a writing discipline, throughout most government departments.

(When I applied for a term job in government some years ago, I was startled to be asked, green and unsworn as I was, if I knew how to write "Cab Docs.")

So there it was for native leaders to peruse, a paper that would make political history, an innocent draft of Rural and Native Housing Policy.

After the meeting Rudnicki said the document mustn't be taken away; the copies were picked up. He explained how many changes still might take place – by the Management, by the Minister, by the Cabinet. He had carried the consultation process as far as he could. And the native group, under Belcourt, were pleased and satisfied.

October 10. Belcourt and Teron would flatly contradict each other in court, over a phone conversation that triggered the explosion.

Belcourt said, *Teron phoned me.* He told me he was meeting the Minister at eleven that morning. I said I was very pleased with the policy and the way we had been consulted. Teron asked me to write a letter to Basford confirming this, and get it to the Minister's office at once. So I did. Gene Rheaume was there in the room and I told him as I got off the phone, and Gene wrote the letter.

Teron said, *Belcourt called me.* He told me he had heard I was meeting the Minister at eleven o'clock, and offered to write a letter expressing satisfaction with the policy. I didn't think I had any right to prevent him. In this conversation I learned to my horror that Belcourt had seen the government document, had been over it clause by clause.

Teron did meet Basford on the morning of October 10. Rudnicki had been called by Teron, and had brought others, but they waited in the hall for over an hour until Teron thrust his head out to say they might as well leave, the Minister had no time to go into the native housing proposal that day.

But behind that office door, what was Basford saying to Teron? Teron said next day, Rudnicki testified, that Basford "blew his stack." The Minister was furious at the thought of taking to Cabinet a proposal seen in advance by native people. He was furious that Belcourt had sent round a letter, indicating that Belcourt even knew the time and place of a meeting between Minister and Corporation president. What kind of a loose operation was this?

Perhaps he threatened Teron's job. Teron would deny all this. His version was that he and Basford discussed the matter in a calm and serious way, after Teron apprised the Minister of what he had just learned with such a sense of shock: the betrayal of his oath of secrecy by Rudnicki, a trusted civil servant, in revealing a Cabinet Document to unauthorized persons.

"I informed him of the call I had just received and this showed the Native Council of Canada had had access to the document. I had no prior knowledge they had seen it – not in any way, shape or form. Otherwise I would not have been so surprised and alarmed. Both Basford and I understood what it meant."

A resignation issue, Teron told Rudnicki next day. Remember Walter Gordon resigning after discussing the make-up of his budget with "outside" economists?

But: "Teron said, 'It's my head or his,' meaning Rudnicki's," another witness would testify. "'The Minister was upset,'" another witness would quote Teron, "Teron said it was a case of Rudnicki or himself having to go."

So did Basford visit his wrath on Teron? Did Teron rush to fire Rudnicki to save his own position? Did either or both of them welcome the chance to get rid of a guy who dealt on equal terms with people like the Métis? Clearly, as the court evidence showed, that was the way it happened.

Like the year 1170 again, and Henry II and the slaying of Thomas à Becket – *"Will no one rid me of this troublesome priest?"*

The larger questions: Why should government papers developing policy for us be kept secret from us? Were these people promised consultation with no real intention of consulting? Does a Minister deal in such hypocrisy?

Robert Marjoribanks, head of information services at CMHC, confirmed, "Walter was caught between the rhetoric and the reality."

What happened immediately after that blow-up ("calm discussion") in Basford's office was that Teron, back at the CMHC building on Montreal Road, had a private session with Lorenz Schmidt, the very young policy drafter who had actually placed the document on the table. They established to their satisfaction that Rudnicki could be held responsible.

Somewhere about this time there was a consultation between Basford, Teron and Gordon Robertson of the Privy Council Office. Robertson's views on government "leaks" were well-known.

Teron summoned Rudnicki on October 11.

"I was still waiting around, expecting to see the Minister since he hadn't had time for us the day before," Rudnicki said.

Teron told him that he had just been informed that a Cabinet Document had been shown to members of the Native Council, and this was "a resignation issue." Rudnicki, unbelieving, protested that what the natives had seen was by no means a final or official Cabinet Document. He refused to resign. He asked Teron to check what had happened with other members of his staff.

Teron, on the witness stand, "I deliberated and sought counsel. When visiting the Minister on another matter I raised the matter, and also with Gordon Robertson."

He called in Jean Lagasse, another staff member in Rudnicki's group; and Lagasse would be one of the witnesses to testify that Teron said, "It's either Rudnicki or me."

On October 12 Rudnicki was called again to Teron's office. In the presence of Eugene Parent, personnel director, and W. Scott, head of the CMHC Legal Division, he was again asked for a resignation, and again refused, saying such a move would be tantamount to an admission of guilt. He was handed a letter of dismissal, for "indiscretion and lack of judgment in showing a Cabinet document to members of the Native Council of Canada," an action which "constitutes serious misconduct."

"I would ask you to leave the building immediately and not to remove any documents from your office or any other office," was the astonishing further wording of this letter to dismiss an eighteen-year veteran of the public service.

Rudnicki was escorted back to his office by Parent and Scott. It must have seemed bizarre. Walter Rudnicki had walked into his office that morning, somewhat "traumatized" by Teron's demand, but still a senior public servant, a $30,000-a-year man, head of a large, key division of a thriving government corporation. He was *escorted* out, asked to empty his briefcase, which contained nothing but a book, and to take nothing from his office. (In the courtroom his confiscated desk calendar with an entry "Meeting with NCC" would be solemnly produced to try to prove that a consultation meeting was held September 20th instead of September 19th.)

Rudnicki called together a half dozen colleagues to go over with him the events of the previous few weeks. Statements were drawn up.

Still not believing the affair couldn't be mended, Rudnicki visited Basford, telling him the media were curious about rumours but were being held at bay, since press reports would surely be damaging to them both – but Basford did not concede that the story would reflect any discredit on *him*. Rudnicki then put it in writing to the Minister, offering a graceful way out, with Rudnicki quietly reinstated but immediately transferred to another government job. Or, Rudnicki wrote (October 29, 1973):

> Another possibility might be to rescind the dismissal pending a full and impartial enquiry into the allegations which have been made against me. If I am cleared as a result of such an enquiry, CMHC presumably would be obliged to reinstate me in my former position and responsibilities. The problem in this option is that such concepts as 'consultation' and 'client involvement' in policy development have entered into the official useage of the public service without

ever being adequately defined in an operational sense
. . . it might be preferable from my point of view to rely
on a judicial process . . .

The judicial process it would be, and it would strike beyond
the simple matter of dismissal to those root questions of
"consultation" and "client involvement."

Ron Basford's reply to Rudnicki (October 31, 1973) appeared at once to uphold Teron's action: "It was accordingly
the President who investigated the events that preceded your
dismissal and who came to the conclusion that, in all the circumstances, they did, in fact require the action that he took in
the discharge of his responsibility . . . " and at the same time to
disclaim his own involvement: "I think it would be quite im-
proper for me as Minister . . . to substitute my judgment for
that of the President." Despite Teron's assertion that he had
gone back to talk again to Basford before Rudnicki was fired.

Rudnicki consulted John Carson, head of the Public Service
Commission, and Gordon Robertson, about other jobs. The
"Dear Walter" letters of reply were sympathetic but vague.
Doors did not open. He had to go west, to Alberta briefly and
then to Manitoba where he found a berth on good terms as a
contract consultant. He commuted between Winnipeg and
Ottawa.

Simone said, "If I hadn't had such good kids, in their teens
too, I couldn't have handled it. Walter would have had to give
it up."

For Rudnicki had decided to take his case to court.

The solicitor he chose was Dan Chilcott, a criminal lawyer,
once a magistrate in the Northwest Territories – which Rudnicki thought might have given him some sympathy with native needs. Chilcott, in court, would be tough and effective,
bearing down hard on unfriendly witnesses, never prolonging
an argument to the point of wearying a patient judge, but
building a strong clear case against the CMHC, against William Teron.

Chilcott told me he'd handled many a "wrongful dismissal"
charge: usually the grounds were as simple as getting drunk on
the job. The implications of this case clearly fascinated him. In

court, he assumed an offhand, casual assurance, scoffing at government pomposity.

"What if 'Confidential' is stamped on a comic book? Does that make it confidential?"

Yes – er – no, said William Teron. Or, perhaps. The judge would find his testimony "astounding."

At stake would be Rudnicki's financial security and his future, vindication if the case went for him, pity soon passing away if he should lose.

Later Simone confessed to me, "I wondered in those days how I would arrange my face if we lost."

In September 1974 CMHC lawyers approached Chilcott to settle out of court. Their offer was "totally unacceptable." Rudnicki pressed his suit.

The Trial

"Who will the judge be?" I asked Chilcott.

It turned out to be Mr. Justice John O'Driscoll. Point of view unknown. *Younger* than I am – what does youth indicate? Might he not still be wedded to the letter of all law and regulation, respect for orthodoxy in his bones?

For apart from Rudnicki's stake in this was much more. What I saw, and the reason why I had begun researching this book, was that we have reached a time when we must expand our democracy or lose it. People must come closer to government, or accept a more autocratic control than we have ever had or believed possible here. If the CMHC won this case it would mean a clamping down throughout government. It would encourage a tighter regime, a sterner discipline, in a government that already wielded too much closely guarded power. Efficiency can always be pleaded for. There are large economic problems ahead: to handle those problems must the government keep *us* outside and uninformed? Some people talked that way. Some people believed democracy was finished, a luxury fit only for easy times.

Several things happened before the case came to court, to strengthen Rudnicki's stand.

At the exact time of the Rudnicki firing Gordon Robertson directed a Privy Council Office administrator, D. F. Wall, to divert a study he was preparing to include a review of the question of government classification of documents. Wall's report was not released for a year: it criticized the system and recommended less restriction.

In May 1975 a situation almost identical to Rudnicki's 1973 meeting occurred when Indian Affairs' officials met members of a National Indian Brotherhood consulting group. A policy proposal labelled "Cabinet Document" was on the table and was passed around. A reporter phoned Rudnicki who commented: "The parallels are interesting . . . " Nobody was fired.

Asked in the House of Commons on July 17, 1975, what a "cabinet document" was, Iona Campagnola, Parliamentary Secretary to the Minister of Indian and Northern Affairs replied briskly that: "a document does not become a cabinet document until it has been approved by the responsible minister, signed by him or her, and forwarded to the Privy Council Office."

People in government who talked to me laughed at the pretext for firing Rudnicki. "It was a trumped-up charge," said Mike McCabe, now an A/DM at Consumer and Corporate Affairs.

The senior people at CMHC were watching through their fingers, even those who fought Rudnicki now privately willing him to win, for an autocratic reshuffling of CMHC under Teron was underway and had reduced morale to low ebb.

But there was some nervousness current. Rudnicki was tense. He said the RCMP had been making interested enquiries about his arrangements in Winnipeg. He thought several times his phone was tapped.

Day One

Courtroom Number Two, in the grey stone pile of the old County of Carleton Courthouse, Nicholas and Daly.

Chilcott is a handsome lawyer, strong-featured, a forward thrust to head and shoulders in the best courtroom style. He's quick, and he is careful not to bog down his argument with too many asides. He is assisted by a member of his firm, William Simpson.

Peter McIneny is the chief civil litigation lawyer from the

Department of Justice, appearing for the defence. Soft brown hair, soft brown beard, unobtrusive glasses, soft voice. A careful presentation always. He is backed up by as many as four legal persons. For much of the proceedings a lawyer or two from CMHC's legal division also looks on. Also aides from Ron Basford's office.

Seated alone or with his secretary, Bill Teron attends almost every hour of the proceedings. His expression varies from jaunty and offhand to sullen.

Rudnicki tugs at his moustache. He, too, is in his place day after day. His son Richard slips in to sit near him, or Simone and their daughters.

Meeting in the corridor outside, Teron and Rudnicki manage the civilities, but quickly seek the support of their respective groups.

Chilcott says his client is suing the Corporation because he was "wrongfully, arbitrarily and without any or sufficient cause, dismissed."

Before the first witness is called they are into the heart of the matter.

For McIneny refuses to have produced in court the documents that Rudnicki was supposed to have distributed. They cannot be entered as exhibits because they are "Confidential"! At the Examination for Discovery in 1974, an affidavit from the Minister attested to their confidentiality and that minor court ruled in the CMHC's favour. The Minister now is Barney Danson. Basford had served his time in Urban Affairs and was promoted in August 1974; he is now Minister of Justice. Danson, perhaps significantly, did not declare the documents inaccessible on the ground that to show them would "violate the confidence of the Privy Council" (one of his options) but merely for broad reasons of "public interest." And he did not use Section 41 (1) (2) of the Federal Court Act which would have been a final decision, but Section 41 (1) (1) which left some discretion to the court.

Now Mr. Justice O'Driscoll must rule on the question.

Simpson requests that the judge take a look at the documents. McIneny says that Danson's affidavit means the public must never see them, though the judge if he so decides may see them.

The judge says "We are on a merry-go-round." He wonders, if the papers are confidential, how can there be a law suit? He reserves judgment on what to do in the matter.

And Chilcott presents his case, first calling Tony Belcourt, swarthy former president of the Native Council who delights the press by saying that when he heard Rudnicki was fired, "I guess I turned white." He talks of the change in the negotiated policy from something he called "garbage" to one he could accept. He describes carefully the telephone call from Teron, and how it was arranged that he would send an immediate letter to Basford's office to strengthen Teron's hand in meeting with the Minister.

In spite of Teron's warning to lay off the Rudnicki case after the firing, Belcourt had taken occasion once when he visited Basford's office, to ask the Minister to intervene. He got no satisfaction.

McIneny's laborious cross-examination brings an interruption from the judge: "What counsel means is, did Teron promise to let you see any document?"

"He promised," says Belcourt, "and we understood, that we would be allowed to review the policy proposal to be prepared by Mr. Rudnicki. Policy papers are policy papers."

After Belcourt, Rudnicki. His career reviewed, his position at CMHC. He is on the stand continuously for a day and a half. He says,

> 'Confidential' we saw on just about everything. There was no firm policy on what it meant . . . I would draft a proposal, it would go to the Management Executive. It might have to come back for revisions, redrafting, as many as a dozen times. When Management was satisfied the president would discuss it with the Minister, there would be a presentation to the Minister, and it might come back to Policy Planning and possibly again to Management or merely through the president to the Minister. He would sign it and it would go on to Cabinet.

Day Two
Rudnicki continuing to explain what a "Cab Doc" is.

"The policy proposals directed at the eventual cabinet document are cast in this form, by way of discipline, presenting the arguments in logical sequence."

Rudnicki's account of successive meetings, successive drafts. Then the first request from the Minister to see the policy proposal, the hurried call from Teron, his angry rejection of part of Schmidt's work, Schmidt dressed down and accused of "manipulating," sent back to repair the document. How they briefly explained to Basford the procedure to that date, received his commendation.

At last, "I thought we would have one final meeting of consultation with the Native Council" on October 5. And the document on the table, and the harmony achieved with the native leaders though the policy was not all they had hoped for, explanation of the fact that Management, Minister or Cabinet might introduce changes later. A *successful* consultation.

On October 11, Rudnicki called into Teron's office and told he must resign. The next day, "the axe."

In the course of Chilcott's presentation, another flurry about producing more papers. Two documents with catchy titles: "Guidance Notes for the Conduct of Cabinet Business – Restricted." (Restricted is one step beyond confidential.) and "Record of Cabinet Decision: Distribution of Cabinet Documents." This second explains the size of paper to use and the procedure for passing around the documents to ministers.

Chilcott has requested them. McIneny says he has instructions from the Privy Council Office not to release them. Again he invokes the Federal Court Act and the right of the Minister to proclaim the documents inadmissable.

At which point, the court having risen for noon recess, Chilcott wheels abruptly on Teron, two rows behind him: "If a Cabinet Minister comes down and says *these* are confidential the government will fall at the next election – ! Get your Prime Minister down for one more trip to Florida!"

Teron, startled, leaves the courthouse. Later the word comes from the Privy Council Office: confidentiality is suspended for those two innocuous documents.

That afternoon, another intervention by the judge. Chilcott

attempts to get Rudnicki to explain, from his experience at the Privy Council Office, what a Cabinet Document really is. McIneny objects. The judge says: "I haven't heard that these 'Cab Docs' got anywhere near the Cabinet. All I have heard is that he is supposed to have shown something he should not have shown . . . "

Are you listening, Gordon Robertson? There is a spurt of excitement. I suppress it. I laugh at myself: it is like hope and refusal to hope before a child's Christmas. Later, despite McIneny's claim for privacy, Mr. Justice O'Driscoll rules that the documents will be delivered to him in a sealed envelope; *he* will then decide whether the needs of litigation outweigh any prejudice to the public interest.

Now Rudnicki is under cross-examination. He has been a long time in the witness box. McIneny takes him again through his entire testimony, lingering on the policy prevailing at the PCO, despite his previous objection to this line of evidence. Rudnicki stands up well, answering from a dozen angles how "confidentiality" is established. "The deputy minister in theory has the power to classify, but in practice the people doing the drafting classify or not, at their own discretion." It was Lorenz Schmidt, well down the line of authority, who actually put the "Confidential" labels on the documents the Native Council saw.

Day Three

Almost the entire day McIneny continues his cross-examination of Rudnicki. The line is obvious: did Rudnicki get authorization from Teron or Basford to show the specific documents? Rudnicki's reply: he felt he had received instructions when both Basford and Teron assured the natives there would be consultation. It had never occurred to him to bring up the specific question of using a particular document at the joint meetings. He assumed they would use the latest draft. "He(Teron) authorized us to share our policy proposals, which were of course written down on paper. The only way I know to consult is to share a paper with them."

He says he did not specifically tell Schmidt to take that draft to the meeting, and this denial becomes one of the points at issue.

Day Four

This is the day that decides what will happen to those "Confidential" documents.

The judge has read them; he has passed them to Rudnicki's lawyer who begins the day's proceedings by saying he can see nothing in them to embarrass the government nor any reason why there should be any restriction on them.

McIneny argues to continue to keep the papers in a sealed envelope. Both sides acknowledge there are no real precedents to this case. But McIneny has claimed it is not in the public interest to show the documents. Here the whole policy of secrecy is being argued, as McIneny realizes, though he protests:

> It is not the policy of the government regarding confidentiality we are debating – a policy it is entitled to maintain, and to insist it be respected and maintained by its employees. This policy goes on regardless of the outcome of this case . . . I can't overemphasize the degree of importance the Defendant attaches to this issue of confidentiality . . .

He mentions its connection to *Cabinet solidarity.*

Mr. Justice O'Driscoll questions McIneny. Is there a card index system at CMHC which controls all copies of such documents? Can McIneny account for every copy?

"Some, I am told, were shredded," McIneny says. But he answers the judge's question: no, he can't account for all copies; there is no complete system or record.

The judge pursues the matter. If he orders the copies in court restricted, how is he to know one may not turn up anyway in some reporter's hands? McIneny has no guarantee.

If he gave an order to restrict the documents, the judge goes on, how would the remainder of the trial be conducted? How would counsel refer to the contents of the documents? "Are you suggesting that we continue on an in-camera basis?"

"A tempest in a teacup!" Chilcott says. "If other copies had been shredded they would have kept track of those shredded, or the system is absolutely useless . . . And, in any case, the policies in these documents are substantially those that were announced by Basford in 1974."

Mr. Justice O'Driscoll reads his decision. Previously he has decided that the papers may be seen by the plaintiff's counsel. Now he must rule if *any* restrictions on their use will be imposed in the course of the trial. He states that the "public interest" attested to by the Minister in his affidavit is not sufficient to impose secrecy on the operation of this court. He reads from the 1913 Law Reports of the British House of Lords, a decision by Lord Shaw of Dunfermline quoting Jeremy Bentham, renowned English philosopher and jurist:

> In the darkness of secrecy, sinister interest and evil in every shape have full swing. Only in proportion as publicity has place can any of the checks applicable to judicial injustice operate. Where there is no publicity there is no justice. Publicity is the very soul of justice. It is the keenest spur to exertion and the surest of all guards against improbity. It keeps the judge himself while trying under trial. The security of securities is publicity.

The judge adds:

> This applies to putting wraps on pieces of evidence in the course of this case . . . It would be an error on my part to order any restriction on these documents. Therefore they will be filed as exhibits like any other exhibit in this court.

Now we breathe, as though it is the first breath of a new season.

There is a brief recess, prolonged by a conclave behind a closed door by Teron and his lawyers. They return to ask that the court be adjourned for a day, "so further instructions can be obtained." McIneny is shaken.

Chilcott objects. "My friend has the resources of the federal government behind him; my client is only an individual. We are holding witnesses brought from Edmonton . . . "

"It is of extreme importance," McIneny says.

The judge says,

> The request is unusual. But this case is unusual, it has some unusual aspects. I am disposed to grant the request, but it seems to me it should be on terms that it was not brought

about by the plaintiff, and that the costs for the day are payable to the plaintiff.

Nothing that comes later can be more significant. The government and this court could be on a collision course. This case will be quoted in other courts, will be dissected in law journals and pontificated on in Parliament and press.

Day Five
Chilcott calls other witnesses. George Whitman, who worked on the native housing policy and is now with Rudnicki in Manitoba, speaks glowingly of the spirit that pervaded the meeting between natives and Basford on the Hill, when both Basford and Teron told the full group there would be a new kind of consultation, step by step.

> As we adjourned, my feeling was that for the first time in many years there had been success in generating a partnership between government and the people that meant something – here was a group of disprivileged people and the minister together working out a program for human betterment. That was the pervasive feeling at the meeting – a mood of optimism and trust. I left with a feeling of great accomplishment.

Whitman is the only witness to go into his feelings on the matter. The other witnesses for the plaintiff, continuing the next day, are Lawrence Gladue, former vice-president of the Native Council; and Gene Rheaume, who headed Rudnicki's task force on native housing, now with the Ontario Association of Métis; Ernie McEwen, a consultant on contract with CMHC, and Jean Lagasse heading the "Native Housing Group" at CMHC in its early stages. Their testimony varies in detail, but confirms Rudnicki's position: positive assurance was given by Basford and Teron to the natives on September 12 that genuine consultation would take place; the headings on documents used at meetings were never discussed because they were irrelevant to the main purpose, which was the substance of the proposals.

Several remarkable comments on the label "Confidential"

come from these witnesses. Gene Rheaume says he used it as a device to get people to read stuff. If it was left off nobody paid any attention to the document. So labelled, it went through "the system" at a faster clip. Jean Lagasse says "The decision to put 'Confidential' on a document is just whenever someone decides he wants to write it up that way . . . I've even seen it stamped on press clippings."

Yet this is the repeated thrust of McIneny: do you recall any authorization to show confidential documents to the native people? Answer, from all: "The question never arose. We knew we were to work together on the policy."

Gene Rheaume backs Belcourt on the significant details of the phone call between Teron and Belcourt. Belcourt had taken the call in Rheaume's office; he had heard most of Belcourt's side of the conversation. Yes, he was sure from Belcourt's manner when he hung up that he had just heard of the meeting to be held in a couple of hours between Teron and Basford. Yes, he was sure the decision had just been taken to write a letter to the Minister praising the policy and the successful consultation. He knew because he, Rheaume, had to write that letter in a rush, make extraordinary arrangements to get it over to Basford's office before Teron would arrive – in time to "do some good." But he had been skeptical: "It struck me we shouldn't have to write the Minister telling him the President was doing his homework."

In cross-examination McIneny presses, "Had you any previous information regarding that meeting at eleven o'clock?" And Rheaume replies, "No. If I'd heard it before I'd have written the letter before."

"Did Belcourt indicate that he'd heard about that meeting before?"

"*No.* He was in a panic as he hung up the phone. He wanted that letter out."

The letter that triggered Basford's temper.

On these two points Teron would flatly contradict Belcourt. Teron's testimony would be that Belcourt must have found out from another source that Teron was going to see the Minister at eleven that morning. "My secretary would have been advised. I don't know whether she had told *Rudnicki*."

Day Seven
We are into the second week of the trial. There is testimony from a personnel officer, and a legal adviser to the Professional Institute of the public service about tenure in office, pension and other rights.

Chilcott concludes his case and it is McIneny's turn at bat. His first witness is William Teron.

Teron affirms that he is now *chairman* of CMHC and also Secretary (deputy minister) to Urban Affairs Minister Danson – an amalgamation is taking place, putting unified control in Teron's hands.

He says: "The concept of Cabinet Solidarity extends to advisers. There is only one policy, that is the government's policy. We can't have advisers revealing a policy which may appear more or less generous, may arouse expectations and be divisive."

The government line of defence.

His version of what was promised by way of consultation: to accept "data" from the natives; then eventually, when Cabinet had approved a policy, to do them the courtesy of letting them hear it first, just before making it public. This is exactly what happened, Teron says, when the policy got on track again and eventually reached an announcement by the Minister in March 1974.

Chilcott, in cross-examination, blisters Teron. Teron cannot decide whether he would consider a comic book stamped "Confidential" confidential or not. He identifies "exactly" the October 3rd Cab Doc, but a moment later cannot recall whether Schmidt, after his reprimand, replaced one page or a whole back section. He leaves the witness stand at noon, dejected.

Chilcott hammers him again. He questions Teron about Lorenz Schmidt who was called in to discuss Rudnicki's misconduct before the firing. Chilcott has been informed at the earlier Examination for Discovery that Schmidt was in a junior position. Teron qualifies that: a middle position. Chilcott thus draws attention to Schmidt's rapid promotion by Teron until now, at age twenty-seven, he ranks as an A/DM.

What does Teron mean, when he says he promised the natives he would continue consultation as in the past? Which they were griping about! Which was nothing!

Teron bridles and retorts: "Some of them complain if we're not a rubberstamp to their position!"

Chilcott pursues: You *had* all their "input." You used the word "consultation." You wanted their views at that time, from that time forward.

Teron says: As we had enjoyed it in the past.

Chilcott: They didn't want it as in the past! Isn't that what Daniels and Spence were objecting to?

Teron: Yes.

Chilcott: You said it would be the same as in the past. And they were *satisfied* with that?

Teron said they were always pursuing that subject. "They wanted to put their elbows on the Cabinet table."

The case begins to build around a very touchy issue. Did Rudnicki specifically discuss with Schmidt the number of copies of that document required for the consultation meeting? For this would be evidence of Rudnicki authorizing the distribution. Here Teron mentions that after the October 3rd meeting with the Minister, *he* rode back, he thought, with Bob Marjoribanks. (Rudnicki says Teron rode back with Schmidt, thus contradicting Schmidt's story of a taxi ride, with Schmidt, Rudnicki and Lagasse in the car, when he was instructed by Rudnicki to get enough copies ready for October 5. If this begins to sound like Agatha Christie . . .) It's a delicate point. Chilcott's questioning seems to point toward a deliberate attempt by Teron (calling Schmidt back from a holiday in the west "just to tell him Rudnicki was fired") to use the junior man in nailing Rudnicki. Rudnicki denies that he gave Schmidt precise instructions, though as Schmidt's superior he "assumed responsibility" once the thing was in the hands of the people at the meeting.

Chilcott pursues: Why did Teron call in Schmidt to find out if indeed the documents had been shown at the meeting? Why not Rudnicki himself? Teron says, "I suppose Schmidt was very vivid in my mind . . . " And Chilcott asks, "Suppose Schmidt was trying to endear himself to you after the blast you had given him?"

Next Teron denies saying to anybody that it was "his head or Rudnicki's." Asserting that those who so quoted him were "incorrect."

Chilcott switches back to that "Confidential" label. Precisely who authorizes it? The answer is nobody. Or anybody. Or "everyone initiating a policy."

So who could order such a label removed? Teron stumbles. There is some incoherence and the judge in compassion intervenes. "Please restrain yourselves. Don't both speak at once."

Day Eight

McIneny calls Michael Pine, yet another member of Rudnicki's group, as witness. But his testimony adds little. And he readily admits to Chilcott that though he understood general practices of confidentiality, "in this instance we were instructed to deal with a group so it was somewhat different." He says however that he "believes the distribution was done at least with his (Rudnicki's) knowledge."

McIneny calls only one other witness, Lorenz Schmidt. The lack of corroborative evidence is significant. Why was not the Minister, Ron Basford, called to back up Teron?

Lorenz Schmidt looks defensively young, nervous. He exchanges a tentative grin with Bill Teron. He tells McIneny in excruciating jargon his positions and responsibilities at CMHC. He was an "analyst" – fresh out of university with a B.A. – in 1973. Reorganization exercise. Structures. Front-end. Schedules. The pipeline. This appears to have an effect on the judge, who instructs him to speak more slowly, since such terms, however familiar to Schmidt, are not known to the court stenographer. Twelve times in a row Schmidt says, "at that point in time." McIneny starts saying it too.

The judge interrupts Schmidt again to ask, after he has reeled off the names of executive officers present at a Management meeting, how he remembers they were all there? The judge discloses that the minutes show only half the officers present. In this and other interventions, Schmidt in his replies fails to address his Lordship with the proper title, as the others have done. He has not been schooled in courtroom manners.

Schmidt gives testimony that Rudnicki *phoned* him about getting copies of the Cab Doc for the October 5th meeting. "There is no doubt in my mind he knew those documents were going to be at that meeting."

In the afternoon Chilcott bears down on Schmidt, leaving him angry and distressed. Yes, Schmidt says, he at a certain stage in its formation decided to put "Confidential" on the document.

Chilcott: Though you received no instructions to?

Schmidt: I also received no instructions not to!

Chilcott: *Answer my question, sir!*

Schmidt: No.

Chilcott reverts to evidence from the 1974 Examination for Discovery, when a statement was given that Schmidt got instructions from Rudnicki about the documents in a taxi ride on October 3rd, with Lagasse in the cab. As soon as Schmidt retires from the witness stand, Chilcott recalls Jean Lagasse, who states that following Rudnicki's dismissal Schmidt tried to get him to "recall" that taxi ride and the instructions, but he told Schmidt he could not. He tells Chilcott now that the only such ride he remembers was a later one, after the aborted October 10th meeting with the Minister, when the October 5th meeting was over and done. There were bad feelings between Schmidt and Lagasse when Lagasse failed to recall what Schmidt wanted. And afterwards Schmidt's story changed to "a phone call."

Chilcott calls a last witness. It is Dorothee Skarzynski, Rudnicki's secretary at the time of his dismissal. Hers is a story of Teron telling her he had been forced to fire Rudnicki, either Rudnicki or he (Teron) had to go. To which she says she answered that it didn't seem fair, and Teron could always buy himself another position with the Liberal party. Teron firing (but not quite firing) her, suggesting there could be a job at a different level, then saying no such job was available, telling her there would be no job for her in future on the executive floor, the personnel director escorting her to her desk to empty it, embarrassed by her flood of tears. "I felt humiliated; he stood over me while I removed my personal effects; I filled up a paper bag. I was crying and upset."

What headlines for Ottawa newspapers.

Day Nine, the final day

The two solicitors sum up. It is McIneny first. His sentences

190

are careful and well-formed. He reconstructs his case. He reaches for precedents in other courts, but they are few and scarcely relevant. It is clear this court is breaking new ground.

But midway through his discourse, Mr. Justice O'Driscoll begins to question McIneny.

"Do you say," he asks, "that the sin of the plaintiff is in the showing of the document or the disclosing of the policy? Suppose he disclosed all the policy but didn't show the document?"

"That would be a breach of confidence."

"How then do you define 'consultation'?"

" . . . a process involving the input of the Native Council of Canada and their problem with a view to letting CMHC have the full benefit of their views . . . The CMHC officials had no authority to negotiate . . . "

Says the judge: "I'm at a loss to know *why* they were meeting. They had presented a brief. CMHC knew their position. Or do you say there shouldn't have been any meetings?"

And then he reads from the Shorter Oxford. "Consult: to take counsel together . . . "

McIneny finds it sticky going. He attempts to give Basford's definition of consultation. An initial presentation of data by the natives. Then, *after Cabinet approval*, then "perhaps" the policy would be *referred back to the Cabinet* . . . "if deemed necessary."

Again the judge asks: "Suppose that at a first or second meeting, someone from the Native Council were to ask, 'What are you going to recommend?' "

McIneny echoes Teron: "Oh, they would like to be involved all the way to the Cabinet! But the CMHC officials should not tell them what the recommendation would be."

"And if the answer had been 'We're not going to tell you,' do you think they would have stayed around?"

"Did they not stay around," McIneny replies, "for the announcement finally in March 1974?"

Later, when McIneny has said: "It is up to all senior officers to respect the confidentiality of advice going to the Minister. This (action by Rudnicki) was a breach of the terms and conditions of employment; dismissal was warranted . . . " the judge goes back to McIneny's definition. He ·asks: "Is it your position that the consultation was to be *after* the Cabinet has made a decision?"

There is a chortle in the audience. The judge looks severely in that direction. I expect it is one of the academics who have been drifting in lately from the Political Science departments of Carleton and Ottawa Universities.

McIneny says, "No, but . . . that is what happens, the Cabinet decides, the natives are advised, then the process in complete. Except that is not necessarily the end of it . . . "

The judge asks, "Are they not at that point announcing to the native people what has been done? A decision has been made. A *fait accompli*."

McIneny defends his point. "We are only speculating about what might happen if the native people were dissatisfied at that point. In fact, the policy has not been altered since March, 1974. The program is working."

"But consultation," the judge asks again, "does not in your view necessarily imply disclosure?"

"It could not," says McIneny. "That would be a breach of confidence."

Mr. Justice O'Driscoll says "Thank you" and continues writing his own notes. And McIneny is proceeding to discuss the damages claimed by Rudnicki.

. . . After this exchange, I know there in no question of the outcome of this case . . . It is an intense feeling. The marrow of my bones sings out. I wonder if others will feel as I do, that here at this moment something of great value came to a point of decision . . .

It is after the noon break. The final hours. Chilcott sums up. He is rapid, yet laconic, undramatic. The entire events are reviewed again.

Teron's testimony about what was intended by "consultation" is out of step with that of all the others. Even Schmidt and Pine said *this* consultation was a different, joint undertaking. No one was called to substantiate Teron's – and presumably Basford's – concept of consultation. If Basford had really had this in mind, then the natives were misled in their expectations – and Basford had "forgotten to tell his underlings" not to proceed with the kind of consultation promised.

Schmidt's evidence changed in the period since the dismissal, as to when and where he got instructions from Rudnicki. "Absolutely unsatisfactory. Most suspect."

Chilcott finishes, Simpson takes up the detailed matter of compensation.

Both solicitors get in a few final jabs. But it is winding down.

And finally the judge says he will reserve judgment for one week.

On July 23 the court meets again. Mr. Justice O'Driscoll is brief: he finds in favour of Rudnicki, and he awards him $18,006.41 in lost pay and fringe benefits. He says it has been "a difficult case."

The decision he hands down runs to more than sixty pages, concluding simply:

> . . . in my view, the plaintiff was merely doing what he had been authorized to do. If in the course of carrying out his mandate the plaintiff did show some error in judgment (which I do not find to be so), in my view such error in judgment was minor and not gross or repetitive."

Throughout, he accepts the testimony against Teron and the CMHC. Through pages, he repeats the testimony of Tony Belcourt, of Walter Rudnicki, of Dorothee Skarzynski, rejecting the testimony of Wiliam Teron.

On the matter of consultation, he writes that if Teron's version of what was intended is correct, the native people might well assume that "white man has spoken with forked tongue."

As for the use of the "Confidential" label, he finds Teron's testimony "absolutely astounding."

It is total victory.

A secretary now at CMHC told me: "In five minutes the news was all over. It was funny too, even those old-timers who had fought Rudnicki when he was here were *jubilant*. But it's all in whispers. Nothing is said out loud. Honestly, it's like a *jail* here."

The media took up Rudnicki with obvious relish. He, at

last, was smiling. But exhausted, winding down slowly. He told the press, about Teron, "Every public servant makes mistakes. I put it down to inexperience."

He went on, "The dichotomy between what politicians say and what bureaucrats do will have to be resolved." He said we must have more openness in government.

He also said he would like to take a position again in the government at Ottawa.

The Ottawa *Journal* ran a headline: "Judge Rules for Rudnicki; Teron 'Wrong' " across its front page.

The *Globe and Mail* said, "The judge discounted the testimony of CMHC president William Teron."

That Friday evening the Rudnickis went to watch the Olympic football match at Lansdowne Park in Ottawa, and afterwards, with a happy but tired group of friends, watched the TV news. Distraught and angry, Teron said into a TV mike that *he* had told the truth. He downplayed the judgment as less than decisive, because Rudnicki had been awarded "only $18,000."

It was not a large settlement. After his share of the legal costs, Rudnicki might clear $10,000, for thirty months' anxiety and an uncertain future. But Chilcott explained that the amount was decided within the constraints of a case of breach of contract by the employer, there could be no provision for punitive damages, it was simply on the basis of money that might have been paid if Rudnicki had been given fifteen months' notice, but less the amount he earned elsewhere in the interval.

Nothing detracted from the verdict, which was clear and absolute. It was not to be measured at a dollar a pound.

And the ten-day interval went by. CMHC had decided not to appeal.

There is one dangling thread left from the trial. Peter McIneny claimed that the native people accepted the policy in the spring of 1974, and "the program is working." That needs examination.

What about Walter Rudnicki's role in all this?

It's uncomfortable for others to live and work near a larger conscience; for this and perhaps for various reasons a few people regard his court battle as a mere exercise in self-interest.

Well, self-interest of course. Rudnicki was a proud man with his career in ruins, his income threatened. That's plain enough.

Modern teachers debunk Runnymede for us, explaining that the barons tackled King John not in the cause of justice for all, but in self-interest. The words are there, however: "to no one will we sell, to no one delay or deny, justice." Some one wrote them down. Debunking is only half our wisdom, I expect.

Give Rudnicki credit. Remember he wrote to Ron Basford well before the case started, conjecturing that his own affairs could probably not be settled easily, because those large ideas of "consultation" and "client involvement" might depend on a judicial process for their resolution. At the least, far-sighted in self-interest.

So be careful, talking about this case. You with your modest conscience may be next to find self-interest coincidental with the advance of justice.

10 Wouldn't They Rather Live in Tepees?

If the Trudeau system is working for the best – this system of inner power, secrecy, pyramidal public service, adversary attitudes, special lobbying – if the government has co-opted all the "best brains" and is taking excellent care of us all – should we worry?

Of course we should, because it is too dangerous to have power concentrated and alternative power weak. I get a very nervous feeling about a government and a Prime Minister who says, as I write (June 1976): "The more we give them (the dairy farmers) the more they want. You'd think they'd at least say thanks but no, they just want more."

Besides insensitivity to dairy farmers in economic plight because of his government's reversal of policy, there is the picture of a Prime Minister grudgingly handing back our money while we're to touch our caps as we say thank you.

This concentrated power behind closed shutters is supposed to be in the interest of efficiency.

But the brutal fact is that the harder they try to achieve efficiency this way, the more they stumble. Let's not wander afield with horror tales of the Anti-Inflation Board or other programs. Let's pick up the story of native housing in Canada. The issue on which Walter Rudnicki was fired in 1973.

At the conclusion of the Rudnicki trial in July, the lawyer for the defence, Peter McIneny, pointed out that a different sort of "consultation" (by announcement) took place after Rudnicki left, and "apparently the native people were satisfied" and "the program is now working."

It was three months after Rudnicki left when, at the Native Council's insistence, a new meeting was held with William Teron present. Tony Belcourt was still president of the Native Council, worried about rumours of disbanding the Policy Planning section of CMHC that Rudnicki had headed, belligerent about what he was still calling "a slap in the face and an insult to us . . . that the person who was going to bat for us, carrying out orders, got the axe."

Belcourt's account of that January 1974 meeting was that Teron presented a forty-page document which was like the old program, from which he intended to formulate a Cabinet Document. The Native Council wanted a chance to consider the program: there must be further consultations before the thing went to Cabinet. By the end of the meeting he says Teron agreed.

"It was a meeting at times bitter, full of frustration," Belcourt said. "It's a confrontation situation now." He believed he came away from the meeting with a commitment from Teron that there would be an opportunity within weeks to look at specific options, and that – of highest importance – if provincial governments would not enter readily into a shared program the federal government would proceed alone.

On January 17, 1974, William Teron was interviewed on television and said that, though the 40,000 units talked about in October hadn't yet been started, "things are starting to pull together very well." He confirmed that there would be further consultation with the native people before the final policy was presented to Cabinet. He did *not* say they would go it alone, without provincial help.

The further consultation didn't take place. What happened next was an announcement in March by Urban Affairs Minister Basford, first to the Native Council representatives and next to the press. The government was committed to its Rural and Native Housing Program. It would be not only for native people but for all low-income people in rural areas and communities of under 2,500 population. (This left out Blind River,

Ontario, population 3000 – with desperately bad native housing.) But because poor whites would be included, the government raised the commitment from the mere 40,000 requested by the Native Council to 50,000 new homes within five years.

It would be operational that year, which was 1974. But it would become operational only on the signatures of provincial governments, who would bear 25 per cent of the cost.

In December, 1974, the Native Council held a Native Housing Seminar in Ottawa.

In the nine months since the program had been announced, "we have learned that a coherent policy really does not exist." Only three provinces, British Columbia, Alberta and Manitoba, had signed.

Only twelve houses had been built.

Delegates said:

Some of our field workers went forward in good faith, gathering applications for the program, only to have them set aside. One such field worker said 'We went into the communities and said these programs were available, and we had the money. Later on we were told by CMHC that they didn't have the money so now we have to go back into the field and tell them otherwise. The people are getting very impatient.'

The provincial CMHC offices and particularly the outlying branches appear to have very little understanding of the R. and N.H. policy – even less than our own housing co-ordinator. When visiting the local CMHC office they don't know what we are talking about.

The people in the Regina and Saskatoon offices do not know about the program. They called me and we called them and eventually we were teaching them their own bloody program.

That's the frustrating thing I find about this Rural and Native Housing Program. They came up with this, they introduced it, they give pamphlets to everybody and the majority of people read it and say 'WOW.' Let's capitalize on the $2,500 grant. And when they go to a CMHC office they just run into a stone wall. You can't do this. You can't do that. It's not workable.

Some local CMHC officials don't agree with the R.&N.H. concept.

Field offices put two people to work on the Rural and Native Housing Program; eleven on AHOP (assistance to moderate-income home-buyers). Most provincial governments were still arguing that they couldn't afford their 25 per cent. Another delegate:

> Can't meet with provincial government or Minister responsible for housing. The one meeting we had with him we got sort of a brush-off and the Minister said there was no difference between Native and Rural and that we have already got a rural policy worked out in the province and he failed to outline it of course.

Let's take a quick side step to that other group, the status Indians, whose bureaucratic mentors are the Department of Indian and Northern Affairs. Since 1960 the Department has spent about $200 million under its housing program for Indians, mostly on reserves. That produced about 41,723 units. Most of the units, though, are poor housing. What can you get for $10,000 these days? That is the size of the grant, the maximum subsidy. Because Indians have very, very low incomes and in many cases no incomes at all, they can't add any money of their own to this government grant. So they get rickety homes, fire-hazard homes, rapidly falling-apart, $10,000 homes. All over the reserves. Or at least to the total of 41,723 houses, which isn't very many spread across Canada.

So when the National Indian Brotherhood made another big pitch for housing, in 1974, they proposed a five-year $400-million program financed by Indian and Northern Affairs.

The Indians were arguing for non-repayable loans. George Manuel, then national president, says that is the kind of deal our government makes with "Third World" underdeveloped nations who have no money to repay. About 70 per cent of the Indian population is unemployed. They and their families live on welfare. Yet they need homes. Sometimes decent housing seems the only sensible place to start to change things, because houses mean better health, they mean work for unemployed people, they mean community action and community pride. A lot more than shelter is involved, though shelter is urgent.

In mid-May 1975, George Manuel and other officials of the National Indian Brotherhood met with people from the Department, who had brought along *their* proposal, having rejected the NIB document of the previous year. Incidentally, the departmental proposal was clearly marked "Cabinet Document" and "Confidential" across the top, just like the one that landed Rudnicki out the door in 1973. This one was not only shown around to the Indians at the meeting, it was easily obtainable by the press.

What the press noticed first, and put in headlines, was the Department's admission that Indian housing at present, and since 1960, is a "costly failure." Now there was a new five-year target of 20,000 homes, at a cost of $20,000 a house. *It would be financed through Central Mortgage and Housing,* with the Indian Affairs Department giving an assist by way of subsidization, but not for the total amount.

There were the CMHC officials on hand at the meeting, with Sam Cormier who is their man in charge of native housing (for the non-status and Métis), explaining how the CMHC program "works."

The Indian Brotherhood did not like the proposal.

For three reasons:

Because *their* proposal had been brushed aside and another substituted, without negotiation.

Because they wanted all Indian programs kept under one department, not lost sight of at Health and Welfare or Central Mortgage and Housing.

But most of all because what CMHC was currently doing for the Métis was *nothing.* Nothing at all. Who wants a share of that?

To the end of 1975, the Rural and Native Housing Program at CMHC completed 410 houses across Canada. Of the 50,000 in five years promised by Basford.

While economists had been happily counting the "upturn"

in "starts" for the total housing industry in Canada, while CMHC press releases had radiated joy at exceeding their targets for multiple housing and even for single housing (210,000 starts of both kinds in 1975) the half million natives in their shacks and tents on the fringes of our happy society got a total of 410 new houses in two years.

None of this went into the northern territories, the Yukon and Northwest Territories, where the climatic conditions would seem to make shelter one of the imperatives.

There were always new announcements of good intentions. In October 1975, when that two-year period was almost up, the new Urban Affairs Minister, Barney Danson, was visiting the north and said at Yellowknife: "I am willing to join forces with the minister of Indian and Northern Affairs, Judd Buchanan, in seeking funds from CMHC and the Northwest Territories to deliver – over a five-year period – the necessary units to meet the urgent needs of northern housing."

He said, "I am determined that here, as elsewhere, we will meet the housing needs of all Canadians."

During 1975 most of the provinces signed the Rural and Native Housing agreements. But no one was putting any muscle into the program.

What was this thing called "sweat equity"? A family to contribute labour instead of money . . . How did that fit into the accounts?

"They're not used to dealing with people with no money," said Roger John, a Newfoundland Métis seconded to Ottawa to work for the Native Council on housing (after taking part in a detailed survey of native housing needs in his own province, which showed only 46 per cent of native families earning more than $50 a month; 71 per cent of their homes heated only by an oil or wood-burning stove; 69 per cent needing emergency repair; 65 per cent just plain "not adequate.")

"I don't *blame* anybody," said nice young Roger John. "The government seems concerned . . . "

Back in Newfoundland they apparently had not yet entered into an agreement. A few houses were getting built: 113, they said, in 1975.

Now a very strange thing happened after 1975 came to an

end. There was a report; there was a budget for the ensuing year. The government began claiming that *3,000 units* had been achieved out of the promised 50,000. A modest start, but not *bad* . . .

I looked in the report, called "Achievements to December 31, 1975" for the figures that add up to 3,000.

There were the aforementioned 410 completed homes: 246 in British Columbia; none in Alberta; 20 in Saskatchewan; 11 in Manitoba; 5 in Ontario; none in Quebec; 15 in New Brunswick; none in Nova Scotia or Prince Edward Island; 113 in Newfoundland.

In British Columbia they had abandoned "sweat equity" and pushed up homes by private white contractors – many are faulty and still unoccupied.

There were 926 units said to be in progress.

There were 1,958 said to be "committed." What does that mean? It does not mean four walls and a roof, within which people can take shelter.

But it does bring the total up near 3000, and it does take care of the budget of $45 million for 1975. And to everybody's delight Barney Danson announced as 1976 began that the budget would be doubled to $90 million for the current year.

Bookkeepers are the big achievers in this operation.

A National Monitoring Committee was set up, including people from the Native Council and from CMHC. It met at Ottawa's Skyline Hotel in February, 1976.

The provincial representatives to the Native Council reported. From the Maritimes: nothing started. A commitment to build fourteen units. Elsewhere: There seems to be trouble getting the provinces to designate the communities; CMHC should exert more pressure. The provinces say they lack funds. A project of nine houses with three under construction. Hope. Disappointment. Concern. The figures didn't tally with the year-end report. They were lower.

Gloria George, national president of the Native Council, submitted a brief. She said, "When it comes to the implementation of the program at the field level the program is, quite frankly, not working. If your regional decision-makers are really interested in our housing problems we see little evidence of it and we think the time has come when you must transfer your commitment to the program to your officials as candidly and as strongly as we are speaking to you.

"Doubling the budget for the next year," she said, "will do nothing to overcome this."

She asked, since Barney Danson and Bill Teron were both handy, if the group couldn't meet with the regional directors and branch managers of CMHC at a meeting in Quebec City later in the month. Mr. Danson said he thought it would be a good idea if it could be arranged, but Teron said there was a very full agenda at Quebec City and he would have to let Ms George know later. She was not invited to attend.

Gloria George has given up. She has resigned her office and returned to B.C. As a parting shot (just after the decision was handed down in the Rudnicki case) she issued a press release. She said:

> There was the Prime Minister at the Olympics calling for a dialogue among Canadians to strengthen Canada. How can such a dialogue take place when sensitive and competent officials like Walter Rudnicki are fired for attempting to undertake a dialogue with Canada's Métis and non-status Indian citizens?
>
> The evidence in the case shows the silliness of a system which allows petty bureaucrats to label documents as confidential, when they are supposed to be engaged in a consultative or, as we prefer to say, a participative process to develop appropriate policies and programs which will achieve results at the lowest cost to the taxpayer.

Correspondence was leaked to me from the Urban Affairs Ministry.

Barney Danson (nice fellow – but no match for Teron) in February 1975 sent a two-page memo to CMHC: "Each time we get into a discussion of native housing . . . I feel an intense sense of frustration. Between ourselves, Indian Affairs and Secretary of State, there seems to be a great deal of money being spent with really limited results." His proposal, aimed at building some houses quickly: to develop a "cadre" of up to a hundred well-motivated native people, with the necessary skills in construction, in organization, in accounting and administration. Twenty at a time, to send them into an area "with all the supporting facilities in place – supplies ordered and ready . . . " Local native people to work with the cadre to build houses. At a second stage, most of the cadre group to move on, leaving a few to help the local natives take over.

On February 19, a memo from vice-president Alain Nantel of CMHC (he has since resigned) to a staff member, Eric Acker. Mr. Teron has looked at Danson's memo. Mr. Teron wants a response prepared, which would "mention that we take the Minister's memo as 'encouragement' for what we are doing, and we welcome his support . . . "

A memo drafted for Teron's signature. It went on for two and a half mealy pages. "Our current problem is that no such team is possible to assemble immediately. Through the existing cadre program we now have the resources to train 50 native cadre officers in 1975. We are becoming keenly aware of the need to recruit and train these people very carefully . . . " It concluded: "The above, while sketchy, may serve as some indication of the various opportunities we are trying to tap and the reason why we are very encouraged by your complete agreement with our objectives and your sharing of our concerns."

Fifty native cadre officers? Where were they? I checked it out with Sam Cormier, head of the Rural and Native Housing Program at CMHC.

The cadre idea had been part of the original brief that Tony Belcourt presented to Ron Basford in September 1973. Accordingly, in 1974 half a million dollars was appropriated for the purpose. It was "vastly underexpended." To be precise, sixteen native people, one to three per province from Ontario west, were taken into CMHC offices for training. After training, "a few" went back to their home communities where nothing much was happening "because the delivery system hadn't yet come into effect." Others stayed on staff at CMHC regional offices.

After that, "a real slowdown" in 1975, when only four trainees were taken on.

In 1976, bright hopes and another half-million-dollar budget. Plans to hire from twenty-three to twenty-six people under the cadre program in the course of the year.

Hardly the story of a program "working," as the counsel for CMHC claimed in court.

In the name of efficiency, what exactly are CMHC's successes?

The CMHC has always regarded itself as a lending institution. Its first duty is to be actuarily sound. Those who borrow must repay. Sound business practice. When *welfare* encroaches CMHC looks askance; it disapproves heartily; its banker's heart is troubled.

So when you bring into view people who are desperately poor and living in squalid, intolerable housing you are introducing something alien. Two diametrically opposed ideas are in conflict: elemental need, and the market demand.

Now the need reaches up to lap at the toes of the upper middle class. It is not only the natives who can't get houses. The only way even a two-income, affluent family can acquire a house these days is to go outrageously into debt. $60,000 buys a bungalow.

The CMHC has never made any real effort to help people acquire homes. CMHC is a back-up to the private mortgage companies and the construction industry. The economists have assured the government that the quickest way to lift the economy out of a depression is to stimulate house-building. This, obviously, has no direct relation to the need for homes – what kind or where. Only to the need to make money building homes, so that builders will build, and their buying and selling will stimulate other parts of the economy. Toward this stimulus function the budget of CMHC has soared to over a billion and a half dollars a year, and if this is the Corporation's function it has been successful. High-priced houses are being built. But an enormous debt structure in mortgage payments hangs over our future. And the proportion of the population that can't manage a decent home is getting larger.

To this bankers' friend kind of CMHC a new element, William Teron, has been added. He has taken over the Urban Affairs Ministry as Under-Secretary of State while retaining control of CMHC as chairman. And thus, while he keeps the purse strings on CMHC's annual budget of $1.6 billion, he gets a grip on *policy* – to influence and direct all urban matters, including transportation, industry location, population movement and growth – whether the policies arise at the municipal, provincial or federal level. Much like Hellyer's dream. But this time under the authority of a very authoritarian man who boasts of his direct line to the Prime Minister.

An extensive reorganization of both CMHC and the Urban Affairs Ministry has followed from a detailed and high-priced (one-quarter-million-dollar) consulting job ordered by Teron from Canada Consulting, the same group that "found" Teron and recommended him for the president's job in 1973.

What he plans to do with this combined and extensive power we can only wait and see.

A CMHC executive still hanging on by his fingernails told me that Teron likes to see himself as a "force of nature" bending the vitally important industrial and financial world of housing and urban development to fit his benign overlordship.

Teron claimed when he was interviewed after his new dual appointment that he had already turned the housing industry around to favour lower-cost houses. Presumably he was referring to the Assisted Home Ownership Plan which assists people with incomes from $10,000 upward. AHOP eats into the public housing program which provides subsidies geared to income, much used by mothers on welfare and others on very low incomes. There are always very long waiting lists.

The high cost of housing in Canada relates to land costs and high interest rates. Both of these, the government could do something about if it would. A report prepared by Peter Spurr at CMHC but just released through a private publisher, "Land and Urban Development" points a stern finger at private developers who now hold almost all the land on the fringe of cities, adding enormously to housing costs. But any suggestion that the government scoop the cream off speculative land profits is rejected by the federal people. The 1976 UN conference "Habitat" urged that "The value added to land by public decision and investment should be recaptured for the benefit of society as a whole." Canada demurred, watered down the resolution to a meaningless phrase.

As for high interest, the government has provided an interest subsidy which means the mortgage companies still get the rate they set, but the taxpayers contribute a bit of it. In vain do we hear an occasional plea for reduced mortgage interest rates for home building (the United States and other countries have taken practical steps in this direction). An Anti-Inflation Board member, John Bidell, startled his colleagues but won no support when he told the Empire Club in Toronto that *he* thought governments ought to bring rates down.

The "approved lenders" backed by CMHC are the banks and trust companies. CMHC protects their interests. It works with large private developers and builders. In these terms it sees its mandate.

One need look no farther than CMHC, its chairman, its policies, for proof of the inability of this high-handed government to meet common problems. If democratic consultation is slow and exasperating, it still works better than this.

11   Late Thoughts

So how is it all to be set right?

Not – necessarily – by defeating the Liberals in 1978. If you've read all this with nothing else in mind you've missed the point. Let's not make the ghastly mistake of throwing out the Liberals in a burst of bombast that is aimed only at letting another group of fellows get to the trough – or, shifting from the barnyard to the machine shop – another group of fellows get their hands on that apparatus of power which the Trudeau administration has created.

Mind you, the temperament of the present Prime Minister has highlighted, if nothing else, the elitist and secretive concentration of power we now have in Ottawa, and does much to disqualify the Liberals as our next government.

What an odd and inscrutable man Mr. Trudeau is! The pleasantest news shot I ever saw of him was as he visited a sheltered workshop for mentally retarded people – I think it was in Saskatoon – and walked among them with such gentleness and friendly encouragement in his manner. Must we probe why he reacts so differently to the legitimate questions of the mentally alert?

So one must say, fighting hard to be properly objective, that a completely reconstituted Liberal party under a new leader *might* have credibility as an agent of change.

As an old believer in the perfectability of mankind I must allow that possibility.

And I propose without hesitation a round of applause to the Trudeau Liberals for so clearly demonstrating the problems of undemocratic government. The firing of Walter Rudnicki climaxed the betrayal of their "participatory democracy" ideal. The court case revealed the ungainly posture of a government walking backwards into the consultative process it had promised, cursing under its breath because the thing was against every normal instinct.

Now the federal government, in the face of mounting public concern over undue secrecy, faces a total challenge to its way of doing business.

What counts now is whether we can find the way to good government. The Rudnicki case was a classic example of what is at stake, and the *kind* of change that is required.

We need to open up new ways of relating to government.

The days when marking a ballot was enough have passed into history. Limiting democracy to the right to vote can bring us very quickly to the point where we vote for the party leader we like best on television – one of the awful options before us now. Vote for the man who "looks sincere" or "seems smart" – and leave the rest to the experts. The swift route to dictatorship. And it's a hard, bloody struggle to get out of that again on the other side.

The new points of contact, which Trudeau tried and failed to establish, are direct links between the people and the government service, the bureaucracy. I don't see how we can escape the conclusion that large reforms are needed in the bureaucratic structure. A decision must be taken to change the principle that the bureaucracy is a support staff to the Cabinet. It must become a sub-structure responsible more to Parliament and less to the Privy Council, and legitimately linked for consultation with outside groups of particular interests and expertise.

Since we have – I think unavoidably – reached a point where much of what we do, own, work at and enjoy is determined by government decisions, we must admit public influence to the making of those decisions. It can't all be done with one mark on a ballot paper at four-year intervals.

Because government is now so large, powerful and complex,

we dare not leave it to operate on its own. It must be opened up all along the line. Punctured to deflate the hot air that suffocates. Ventilated to let in the air from outside. Opened to the light of publicity.

Governments need to make renewed fresh contacts with us in all kinds of ways. If they don't they resort to self-stimulus, both unreliable and sterile.

Two heads are better than one. The proof of the pudding is in the eating. New mottoes for government wallspace. An outside opinion can sometimes spot a silly mistake before it happens. A layman with practical concerns can sometimes make an inspired and creative proposal. Outsiders can also contribute a lot of dumb and selfish ideas. But as long as we all know where the final responsibility rests – in our elected Parliament – the nonsense can be patiently sifted out. I don't think there's any question at all that we'd get ahead *faster* with many opportunities for democratic input. Governments that protest are far less concerned with speed and efficiency than simply with having their own way.

Nor is it any good just throwing spitballs at the present bunch of bureaucrats. John Carson, former chairman of the Public Service Commission, came hotly to the defence of the civil service in his retirement speech (even though he had had some rather nasty things to say about the "slobs" in some departments on earlier occasions). Maybe the *malaise* in government, he said, is just part of the *malaise* everywhere. And the current crop of bureaucrat jokes that has taken the pressure off the Newfies may be funny but unfair.

Q. How does a bureaucrat wink? *A.* He opens one eye.

The general malaise of which Carson spoke is considerable, because we seem to have to rethink the distribution of income, jobs and power – which covers almost everything. Premier Ed Schreyer's provocative statement about aiming for a society where nobody makes more than two-and-a-half times the income of anybody else may have been foolhardy but it sure opened up a lot of discussion. Jobs – any old jobs, or *real* jobs? – is the question that follows hard on the heels of our dedication to full employment. (The conflict between killing baby seals – and jobs. Between growing tobacco – and jobs. Between pollu-

211

tion through plastic containers – and jobs.) But neither income distribution nor work distribution is nearly as hard to resolve as the distribution of power.

The only safe way to go is toward more, not less democracy.

Toward this end we must make the bureaucratic structure of government responsible to Parliament, not to the party in power, and we must insist that it belongs to *us* – to Canada. Not to the Liberals or any other party. The bureaucracy must be our agent, operating in our interests, not our adversary. (What an incredible idea to have inserted itself into government minds!) This means going back to an earlier ideal, which actually has been honestly perceived in various times and places, but not in Ottawa today.

Harold Laski once wrote of a discussion over dinner with Prime Minister Ramsay MacDonald in the early 1920s, when the first Labour government of Britain had been elected, to the horror of all good Conservatives and Liberals. It was a revelation to MacDonald on taking office to discover "the absolute loyalty of the Civil Service which worked in amazing harmony under entirely novel circumstances," he told Laski.

Tommy Douglas, when the CCF first took power in Saskatchewan in 1944, reacted against the blatant patronage of the old regime by pledging that no civil servant would be fired as long as he or she proved capable in the job, and he says he is satisfied that, with a few exceptions, his confidence was not misplaced. Douglas built up one of the finest public administrations we have ever had in Canada.

Mike Pearson in his *Memoirs* said, in describing his assumption of office in 1963 after Diefenbaker's defeat:

> I was very careful, however, not to consult any of my close friends who had remained in the civil service. I never brought them into my political problems, however tempting the prospect. Very conscious of the fact that I had been a Deputy Minister myself and that no other government in Canada's history had ever included so many ex-civil servants, I wanted to make sure that I did not associate with them in any way which would leave me open to accusations that the bureaucracy was advising me on purely political

matters. Early in my administration I called a meeting of all those of Deputy Minister rank to speak to them about the change of government; to thank them for their impartial service over the past years, including those of the previous régime; and to encourage them to continue in that fine tradition. I have heard a lot of talk in recent years that the civil servants dominate the politicians. It was not so in my time in the civil service, and it was not so in my day as Prime Minister. I know they have great power but, in my experience, they also have a very real sense of the meaning of parliamentary responsibility. The danger is that, in spite of themselves, they may usurp functions which are really parliamentary and political. This danger has increased, not by design but almost by accident or default.[1]

The neutrality of the public service relates to the job, and does not require the neutering of men and women. Public servants must be allowed to be real people, not shadows behind a screen. We must know them by name for what they do. They must be permitted to enjoy the same civil rights as people in other jobs. They must not be muzzled, hobbled, or confused about their loyalties. They are hired to serve Canada.

A good public servant will as readily answer questions about his work to an Opposition MP, a backbencher on the government side, or you or me. The only restrictions on what he can tell must relate to national security and defence (leave the opening up in that field for perhaps another century), or to individual privacy where facts have been required by government (as for income tax).

A government employee takes direction from the Cabinet, but decision-making is delegated and visibly delegated, so everybody knows how far he or she is supposed to go, and the range of responsibility that goes with the job. Is that so impossible? I think only our present fetish about streaming all authority to the Cabinet for the sake of Cabinet Solidarity makes it *seem* impossible.

[1]*Mike: The Memoirs of the Rt. Hon. Lester B. Pearson, Vol. 3.* University of Toronto Press. 1975. p. 89.© University of Toronto Press 1975 Toronto and Buffalo.

The skeleton framework on which government hangs is financial – the spending of our taxes. The finances of the nation should be more clearly scrutinized and controlled by Parliament – too much of this has slipped away. The Commons was established to mete out the money required by the king. This was and is the essence of its power. Within the financial framework the spending should be accounted for transparently: we should all be able to see where the bloodstream flows: public accounts should be designed to reveal in the plainest terms what things cost. Because it's our blood – our money.

. . . Let me tell you one last tale, about the National Advisory Council on Voluntary Action. It was set up by the Secretary of State, Hugh Faulkner, at the end of 1974. It was to run for two years. It got fifteen members appointed from across Canada, and two well-paid full-time executive people with well-equipped offices and a support staff of two. In the beginning it seemed to have nothing substantial about it except its name, and that impression became more marked as time progressed. It met every six weeks, and on those occasions the fifteen members were each paid $125 a day plus travelling expenses.

Twelve months later they had a special little seminar, calling in social scientists, to determine what "voluntarism" is.

By spring 1976, eighteen months along the way, it had "defined its task." It submitted an interim report to the Minister. This report protested that it hadn't been dallying; it now knew for sure what it was supposed to do: to wit, submit a report to the Minister in December 1976 with recommendations on how the federal government could help voluntary associations. It asked for more money – an extra $120,000 – because it had now decided which research projects it wanted to undertake (about eight of them, finding out things like what organizations now get financial aid from government), and these research projects would have to be contracted out. However they would end in a burst of speed: the research would be done in a couple of months over the summer, the report would be written up in the fall, translated into the other official language, printed, and absolutely positively presented to the Minister in December. Oh yes, sorry about the slow start.

They got the mandate to carry on, though their request for additional money was cut. No one wanted to admit what a waste of time it all was. And this could be duplicated by hundreds of other examples.

It is no less than criminal that a person earning $6000 a year has to pay taxes into this kind of thing. But when it happens it should not be buried away because it might reflect politically on the Minister. The public servants who made the recommendation or decision should be held to account ...

I suspect there would be a sigh of relief that would rend the heavens over Ottawa if public servants did know precisely the range of their authority and discretion, and if they knew that abuses would be exposed, and diligence in the public interest rewarded.

We must also, for the sake of morale, get back to the merit system in hiring and promoting civil sevants. The system has been wrenched out of shape. It's still the only safe procedure to follow. We must eliminate the distortions – the extra points, in job competitions, for things not related to merit.

On my first application for a job in the public service I resented the "veterans' credits," which meant that anyone who had been a member of the armed forces got an advantage over me. I still resent it. And I resent extra credits for women or for native people or for any other category. The job itself should be clearly defined in terms of qualifications and experience required. And no one should get an advantage based on anything but merit. All the safeguards of appeal procedures and the protection of public service unions are needed so the system can be seen to be fair.

Political staff ("aides" or whatever) for Ministers and even the Prime Minister should be clearly distinguished from the public service and should not be listed in the government phone book. These staff members occupy themselves with relations between an elected individual and his or her constituents and party, and that is not the job of running the country. We're supposed to make this distinction now. We should be making it in fact as well as in theory.

The Privy Council Office and Prime Minister's Office should revert to secretariats, leaving policy-making to the departments of government and ministries. Co-ordinating inter-departmental committees are increasingly necessary, but a secret chamber of executive power is not.

Departments of government should forget the mistaken attempt to imitate "good business management." They should be geared to service. When a service institution becomes lazy and complacent the cure is not to turn it into a managerial wire cage. This is repressive rather than curative, and doesn't work. Turn the floodlights on it, name the people in it, let those citizens affected by the incompetence see inside and voice their wrath.

Probably the most far-reaching of these requirements to regenerate the public service is the proposal to place it clearly and constitutionally under the authority of Parliament. Parliament should scrutinize how the nation's money is spent. Parliament should have the duty of overseeing bureaucratic structures and behaviour.

The institution of the public service should be by law the responsibility of Parliament. The direction of the work of the public service should be the responsibility of the Cabinet.

We might in this way restore to Parliament the supremacy it ought to have. And it would do a lot to shake the wrinkles out of the public service.

Your Business
Three points of contact.

The first, through political parties.

Now that we are moving in the direction of controlled and exposed funding of parties, so that special backroom interests are to carry less weight, the voice of party members should be raised loud and clear. Members should demand sober definition of party policy. They should reject the cult of a leader, especially a leader who wants to keep his cards close to his chest and not reveal "his" policies. They're *your* policies too.

Through political parties the overview, the general direction of affairs, should be determined.

The second, through the public service as it elaborates the chosen policy of the Cabinet.

Policy in full detail can only be designed in relation to experience in governing. So policy formulation mostly has to take place inside the public service, as it does now.

This process should not be secret, but should be conducted openly, with a standing invitation to the public to submit views. Consultation with those outside should be a constant part of the process, as new policies, programs and legislation take shape. The Cabinet of course initiates and in the end approves the policies drawn up, on request, by public servants who are expected not to rely on their wits alone, but on consultation with the general public.

The final authority is the authority of Parliament, most especially in voting funds.

Even the making of budgets should be as open as possible. It would make for a much more cooperative citizenry if people had some understanding of the financial options open to the government. Let people worry a little in advance about how the money should be raised to meet the needs of the country.

Consultative groups. What kind?

First rule, they should never be appointed by the government. They should be independent, firmly touching earth. The shaky sub-structure of appointed groups now clinging to the government on all sides might as well be firmly dismantled. Citizen advisory groups must spring up naturally as the third power in our governing system: the first of course being Parliament, the second the departments, ministries and agencies of the Crown.

A recent proposal by the Canadian Labour Congress points to one move in this direction. In March 1976 the CLC passed a Manifesto that asked for a new place for them in the economic planning which seems likely to go on after the present controls' program ends. Apparently the CLC wants a consultative body to influence economic development – all such matters as the direction of investment, interest rates, trade relations – and it wants to be part of that body in a permanent way along with business management. The CLC feels that it is closest to representing the people in the economy, whose cooperation must be won to achieve economic goals. Such consultation is in effect in West Germany and in Sweden, apparently with results that are both stabilizing and creative.

Because it has never been done in Canada, where the government relies heavily on advice from business but gives labour only a token place, quite new possibilities are opened up. The most critical decisions – provided the government can be persuaded that labour really should be admitted on equal terms with business – would have to do with how far, or how high up the ladder, such consultation goes. In William Teron's immortal words, nobody can put his elbows on the Cabinet table except the Cabinet. An immediate problem is to convince the government and the country that that is not what the CLC has in mind.

Consultation on vital economic problems should of course become a permanent feature of our system, because surely nobody doubts by now that economic planning and a lot of government economic management is shaping up ahead. The dream of lifting controls and suddenly finding ourselves a half century back in time, when the family business and corner store were supreme, is too light-headed to be indulged in. I think we'll be a lot safer, in the large-scale economic decision-making that has to be done, if labour, which is so much closer to the bread-and-butter needs of people, is a partner with business management in the consultation that has to take place.

It may be that some such body as the Consumer Association of Canada should also be admitted to this top-level economic advisory group.

But even if this comes to pass, it's just for openers.

Government departments should actively seek out suitable consultative sources. There should be room for legitimate organizations to connect with the department of government designing policies that affect *them*.

"Legitimate organizations" takes some defining. Offhand, I'd say those organizations should have a visible base in a community of interest, and should be sustained to at least some degree by their own members. Even if it's only a nickel-a-month membership fee. Nothing like a financial stake to make a member keep a sharp eye out, and to keep officers of the group responsive to the rank and file. Money is a great regulator, like prune juice.

The grant-giving practices of government to assist citizen

groups should be scrutinized by Parliament, and subject to a published register. Grants are probably necessary as long as personal income is as unequal as it is in Canada today.

Along with this should go a register of lobbyists, with public disclosure of their client lists. This is *not* private business, it is very much part of the public business. Anyone who hires himself out as a go-between for a client seeking access to government should have to do so up a floodlit walkway.

Anyone should be able at any time to request and receive records of interventions by citizens to government departments.

I believe we must also seek out ways to equalize, or democratize, these interventions and consultations. Simply to acknowledge their legitimacy and usefulness, to declare it an acceptable practice for public servants to consult citizen groups, is a brave first step. Then we must immediately move beyond to regularize the process, until citizen consultation is as fair a process as universal suffrage. Determining what standards can be struck to achieve this goal is a vital task, requiring much skill and experiment.

We can quickly appreciate the objective – that *numbers* of people directly affected must outweigh special privilege. How to categorize citizen groups to reflect this principle is not so easy. People form groups in varying combinations. Perhaps the most common are vocational groups. Lawyers, dairy farmers, librarians – these are producer groups with obvious joint concerns, and with every right to "input" where government policies affect their work. But other associations as well – let us begin to ask the questions about citizen groups which are in a sense consumer oriented – in that they are concerned with the availability of goods and services – from national wildlife parks to passport changes. This kind of "consumer" group is the least organized, but in a long-term sense, surely the key to our extended democracy. The influence of such groups on policy formation would tend toward an economy geared to supply the kind of hats people want to wear, instead of the making of hats as a way of providing wages. Slowly we are shifting toward recognition of consumer groups. The signs are apparent, and encouraging.

The third point of contact is with the bureaucracy as an administrator of programs. The bureaucracy calls it "the delivery system."

Whether it's day care centres or milk subsidies. It seems almost impossible to avoid mistakes if you don't have some sharing of this administrative function with the people on the receiving end. Again this calls for organizations set up by interest groups. Sometimes, no doubt, the same groups mentioned above as contributors to policy-making.

I don't believe government should hand the delivery system over to these groups, who are very apt to get the notion they should be given the money plus *carte blanche* to run a public program. It's collective money, government money, and therefore the government must have a responsible hand, in its actual distribution. But it's not impossible to see this done cooperatively, as a great deal of the distribution of government handouts is done now, with local bodies playing an important role in deciding how the money can be used to best advantage.

The Hordes Without

Now just a cheery note for the bureaucrats who may see nothing but bleak ruin in these proposals. The upper classes who witnessed the advent of universal suffrage suffered similar tremors. And look how it turned out! About one in every three persons doesn't bother to vote, preferring to leave all that tedious business to somebody else. And that's his privilege. If he's content to have things done to him without having a say in the matter, that's his problem. In this country no one is compelled to vote, compelled to join a political party, or ought to be compelled to join any association. If it makes you feel better somehow to stay aloof from it all you may do so, and you still keep the inalienable right to grumble. Can't ask much fairer.

It will comfort the bureaucrats to know that often we (on the outside) will have more trouble organizing and maintaining these free associations of advising groups than the government has had up to now fending them off.

Let the opportunity be there. Let them know their input counts. That could make the difference between an apathetic and cynical public and one that "participates."

What will make it possible to build this triple-jointed democracy is the tremendous thrill and personal satisfaction to be found in mobilizing a group to advance or defend some social need, with some prospect of success. That's the motivation we need to bring people to the point of meeting with government to put forward their views. Afterwards, partly satisfied, the group may subside or even fade away. That's fine.

We have gardens to tend, dollars to earn, babies to pick up and put back to bed, men or women to fall in love with. Everyone has a lot to attend to, and public duty is only part of it.

But it should be taught in school and at our mother's knee that there's no such thing as a free lunch. The things we think government should do for us we must in the final analysis do for ourselves.

It's no good trying to wipe out the collective world. We've got to learn how to collectively control it.